Bill Jones takes us from "puzzled" to "p[...] overview of the Old Testament. Bill's pass[...] foretold in history, and God's plan to reach [...] are what make this a unique and valuable resource for anyone wanting to know God in a deeper way. Don't give up on the Old Testament. Let *Putting Together the Puzzle of the Old Testament* fill in the big-picture for a lifetime of insights into the Bible Jesus read.

CLAUDE HICKMAN, AUTHOR OF *LIVE LIFE ON PURPOSE*

Bill has taken over 1,000 pages of seemingly confusing text from 39 separate books, spanning thousands of years of history, and transformed it into a concise, comprehensive, and wonderfully engaging overview of the Old Testament. The completed puzzle reveals two astonishing Old Testament discoveries: God's love and focus for all nations, and the clear and powerful presence of Jesus Christ.

CHRIS GOODALL, CHAIRMAN AND CEO,
CONTINENTAL AMERICAN INSURANCE COMPANY

Putting Together the Puzzle of the Old Testament is the answer for those seeking to expand their grasp of the Old Testament. Beginning students with no previous Bible knowledge will find a good foundation on which to build. Readers who know many of the stories but do not comprehend their relationship to one another will see how they all fit together. All will appreciate Bill Jones' simple, warm approach to the study of the Scriptures.

DR. BRYAN BEYER, AUTHOR OF *ENCOUNTERING THE OLD TESTAMENT*

Bill Jones demonstrates his passion for God's Word in a way that might surprise you. Often "passion" is mistaken for emotion. That is not what I mean. Bill's passion comes through in his deep understanding of the scriptures, his love for the Author, and his desire to extend His Kingdom to every person in every people.

GREG PARSONS, EXECUTIVE DIRECTOR OF US CENTER FOR WORLD MISSIONS

PUTTING TOGETHER THE PUZZLE OF THE OLD TESTAMENT

Bill Jones

Authentic

ATLANTA • LONDON • HYDERABAD

Authentic Publishing
We welcome your questions and comments.

USA   1820 Jet Stream Drive, Colorado Springs, CO 80921
        www.authenticbooks.com

UK   9 Holdom Avenue, Bletchley, Milton Keynes, Bucks, MK1 1QR
        www.authenticmedia.co.uk

India   Logos Bhavan, Medchal Road, Jeedimetla Village, Secunderabad 500 055, A.P.

Putting Together the Puzzle of the Old Testament

ISBN-13: 978-1-932805-94-9

ISBN-10: 1-932805-94-X

Published in 2007 by Authentic

Cover design: Paul Lewis

Interior design: Angela Lewis

Proofreading: Dana Carrington

Printed in the United States of America

DEDICATION

To the many businessmen of Columbia, South Carolina, who not only allow me the privilege of sharing with them what I learn from the Scriptures, but also faithfully encourage me to seek daily to walk in a manner worthy of our Lord. May we give our lives to impact both our city and the nations with the message of God's love and forgiveness found in a personal relationship with Jesus Christ, the Messiah so long prophesied throughout the Old Testament.

CONTENTS

PREFACE   XI

INTRODUCTION   1
   How the Old Testament is Put Together

ERA #1   17
   The Human Race Out of Nothing
   (Genesis 1 – 11)

ERA #2   33
   The Hebrew Race Into Something
   (Genesis 12 – 50)

ERA #3   49
   Exiting Egypt
   (Exodus – Deuteronomy)

ERA #4   69
   Entering Canaan
   (Joshua – Judges)

ERA #5   89
   United Kings Stand
   (1 Samuel – 1 Kings 11)

ERA #6   113
   Divided Kings Fall
   (1 Kings 12 – 2 Kings 23)

ERA #7   137

Scattered Judah

(2 Kings 24 – 2 Kings 25)

ERA #8   163

Gathered Judah

(Ezra – Nehemiah)

CONCLUSION   187

Admiring the Puzzle's Border

APPENDIX ONE   207

The Reliability of the Old Testament

APPENDIX TWO   213

Old Testament Book Summaries

PREFACE

For the last twenty years I have lived my life in two very different worlds: one very small but extremely deep, the other very broad yet not nearly as in-depth. The first world originates in the classroom where I serve as a professor at Columbia International University, a Christian campus known for preparing grads and undergrads with a deep understanding of God's Word so they can make a difference in the over 100 countries in which they serve.

The second world results from serving with Crossover, a missions agency that focuses on starting churches where no churches exist in Eastern Europe, Central Asia, and North Africa. Rarely does one find a person who has even a rudimentary knowledge of Scripture in these parts of the world.

My dual citizenship, so-to-speak, motivates me to look for ways to give people unfamiliar with the Bible as much information as I possibly can, yet in such a way that they can remember it and build upon it in the future. *Putting Together the Puzzle of the Old Testament* seeks to do just that by dividing biblical history before the coming of Christ into eight eras: nothing/something, exiting/entering, united/divided, and scattered/gathered. If going through this book gives you a better grasp of the Old Testament, then the book's purpose has been fulfilled.

Over the years I have consulted many books written about the Bible. If a similarity exists between any of those resources and this one, please do not consider it intentional. Instead please view it as a compliment reflecting the enduring influence another may have had in my own understanding of the Old Testament.

INTRODUCTION

HOW THE OLD TESTAMENT IS PUT TOGETHER

Intimidating! Overwhelming! Totally confusing! Descriptives such as these suggest how we often feel when it comes to the Old Testament. No wonder, with eight to nine hundred pages of names like Melchizedek, Mephibosheth, Meshelemiah, and Michmethath, who wouldn't feel this way? For the poor soul who happens to start reading in 1 Chronicles, he might even dare to scream, "What's the point?" since the first nine chapters consist of nothing but names like the above.

Not only that, but few churches offer classes that provide an overview of the Old Testament. Those that do seem to make them so complicated that you lose the big picture. As a result, most people miss out on the incredible blessings the Old Testament offers.

If the Old Testament were one of those thousand piece puzzles, then this book provides you with the puzzle's box cover so you can understand what you are assembling. It also helps you put together the four corners and all the straight-edged pieces so you have a completed border of the puzzle. Armed with these advantages, in the future when you read or study Old Testament stories, you will understand how they all fit together. Even if you have no previous familiarity with the Old Testament, that's okay. This book, using easy to understand terms, will help you assemble a tremendous amount of information in a way you can comprehend and remember as well.

Let's begin by looking at the picture on the front of the puzzle box.

EXAMINING THE BOX COVER

Most people think the Old Testament focuses on subjects like the Ten Commandments or maybe the Jewish people. Although we see these subjects again and again throughout the Old Testament, they do not come close to completely describing its contents.

Once assembled, the puzzle pieces of the Old Testament produce a picture of God and His glory. The picture it paints, however, does not resemble the picture of God in the minds of most people. Many think that the *New* Testament reveals a loving God, but the God of the *Old* Testament is one of wrath and vengeance. This mental picture of God could not be further from the truth. The God of the Old Testament is no different from the God of the New Testament. Throughout both parts the Bible demonstrates God's love for man and His judgment toward disobedience.

When put together properly the puzzle pieces of the Old Testament display a picture of God receiving glory by restoring fellowship between all people groups and Himself through His Son, Jesus Christ. You perhaps mistakenly thought that we see Jesus only in the New Testament. Interestingly enough, we discover Christ at the very beginning of the Bible. This makes assembling the puzzle pieces all the more meaningful. It also may have surprised you that God sought to reach all people groups even in the Old Testament. Most people think that His interest in Gentiles doesn't happen until the New Testament. Not so! God's heart has always called to all the nations of the earth. This divine longing will become clearly evident as the outline of the puzzle begins to take shape.

Knowing what the puzzle looks like when completely assembled readies us to open the box and pour the pieces out on the table.

FINDING THE CORNER PIECES

After emptying a puzzle box of its contents most people take time to arrange the pieces in some kind of order. We will do the same. Our puzzle consists of thirty-nine pieces, or what we call the books of the Old Testament. Let's place the pieces in the order you find them in your Bible's Table of Contents. Starting with Genesis and ending with Malachi gives the following list.

Genesis	2 Chronicles	Daniel
Exodus	Ezra	Hosea
Leviticus	Nehemiah	Joel
Numbers	Esther	Amos
Deuteronomy	Job	Obadiah
Joshua	Psalms	Jonah
Judges	Proverbs	Micah
Ruth	Ecclesiastes	Nahum
1 Samuel	Song of Solomon	Habakkuk
2 Samuel	Isaiah	Zephaniah
1 Kings	Jeremiah	Haggai
2 Kings	Lamentations	Zechariah
1 Chronicles	Ezekiel	Malachi

After bringing initial order to the pile of seemingly unrelated puzzle pieces, next we need to find the corner pieces. To discover the corners of the Old Testament, you need a pen or pencil.

Using your pen, group the following pieces into three different boxes. Draw the first box around these books: Genesis, Exodus, Leviticus, Numbers, and Deuteronomy. Group these books into a second box: Job, Psalms, Proverbs, Ecclesiastes, and Song of Solomon. Finally, draw the last box around these books: Isaiah, Jeremiah, Lamentations, Ezekiel, and Daniel. (It may help you to actually do this in your Bible.) If you draw your boxes correctly, each box should contain five books. Notice that two groups of books remain outside of the three boxes. These two groups also contain the same number of books, twelve.

Jump for a moment to the New Testament and look at something Jesus said on the last day of His resurrected ministry. Luke 24:44 says, "These are My words which I spoke to you while I was still with you, that all things which are written about Me in the Law of Moses and the Prophets and the Psalms must be fulfilled." This statement gives us a clue as to how to begin organizing the books of the Old Testament.

Jesus divides Old Testament Scripture into three categories. One category contains the books of Moses, another the books of the prophets, while the last holds the Psalms. Elaborating on these categories allows us to organize the Old Testament books around the following three corners.

The first seventeen books, Genesis to Esther, make up what we will call the **Historical Books** of the Old Testament. We call them historical, not in the sense that the other twenty-two books are not historically true, but in the sense that these seventeen books chronologically tell "His-story" from creation to the years before the coming of Christ.

The Historical Books consist of two subgroups. The first five books contain the Law of Moses. These books, written by Moses and often called the Pentateuch, cover a span starting with creation and lasting until the Hebrew people stand ready to enter their Promised Land which we know today as the country of Israel. The next twelve books, which have no special name like the first five books, complete the historical time line. They begin with the book of Joshua and end with the book of Esther.

The next five books, Job to Song of Solomon, comprise the **Poetical Books** of the Old Testament. Job teaches us how to respond to suffering.

Three Categories of Old Testament Books

17 HISTORICAL BOOKS	5 POETICAL BOOKS	17 PROPHETICAL BOOKS
First five called the Law or Pentateuch		First five called the Major Prophets

• Genesis	• Job	• Isaiah
• Exodus	• Psalms	• Jeremiah
• Leviticus	• Proverbs	• Lamentations
• Numbers	• Ecclesiastes	• Ezekiel
• Deuteronomy	• Song of Solomon	• Daniel

Next twelve called History		Next twelve called the Minor Prophets
• Joshua		• Hosea
• Judges		• Joel
• Ruth		• Amos
• 1 Samuel		• Obadiah
• 2 Samuel		• Jonah
• 1 Kings		• Micah
• 2 Kings		• Nahum
• 1 Chronicles		• Habakkuk
• 2 Chronicles		• Zephaniah
• Ezra		• Haggai
• Nehemiah		• Zechariah
• Esther		• Malachi

The Psalms put the spotlight on proper worship of God. Most people associate Proverbs with wisdom. The book of Ecclesiastes points to living a life of significance by showing how much of what we do leads to vanity or emptiness. Finally, the Song of Solomon speaks about true love. These five topics have captured the interest of man's heart for millennia.

	HISTORICAL BOOKS	POETICAL BOOKS	PROPHETICAL BOOKS
TITLES	Genesis to Esther	Job to Song of Solomon	Isaiah to Malachi
NUMBER	17 Books	5 Books	17 Books
FOCUS	Past	Present	Future
SUBJECTS	8 Times of "His-Story"	5 Topics of Interest	5 Types of Prophecy

The last seventeen books fall into the category of the **Prophetical Books**. These books deal with the future of various people groups, particularly the Hebrews. The prophecies found in these puzzle pieces divide into five different types. Some prophecies speak to Israel's situation during a specific period of her history. Others predict the exile of the nation, while still others point to the nation's return. The rest prophesy either the first or second coming of Christ. All prophecies except those concerning the second coming of Christ have been fulfilled.

As with the Historical Books, the Prophetical Books also consist of two subgroups, the Major Prophets and the Minor Prophets. Whether a book has the major/minor designator attached to it results not from the importance of the prophet or the significance of his message, but rather from the length of his writings.

LOOKING FOR STRAIGHT-EDGED PIECES

Now that we have found the three (not four!) corners, we need to connect them. To do so we need to find the straight-edged pieces. Assembling these pieces produces the border of the puzzle. To find the straight-edged pieces for the Old Testament, you only need to look in the Historical category of books. By looking there, you find all but four (thirteen total) with straight edges. These thirteen trace God's great plan from the beginning of the world until the years prior to the coming of Jesus Christ. If these thirteen provide the content of what God did, then the other four give us a colorful commentary.

So what kind of story do these thirteen books tell?

Genesis portrays two major parts of the story. It begins by telling of the creation of man and why he needs his fellowship with God restored. Continuing the story, Genesis focuses on the beginning of the Hebrew nation, revealing that a Messiah will come from this nation who will bless all the other nations.

Another major part of the story occurs in Exodus through Deuteronomy. These books explain how God delivers the Hebrews from their captivity to the Egyptians. Once free from their former captors, God gives them the Ten Commandments and instructs them on how He wants them to worship Him.

HISTORICAL CONTENT	HISTORICAL COMMENTARY
Genesis	Ruth
Exodus	1 Chronicles
Leviticus	2 Chronicles
Numbers	Esther
Deuteronomy	
Joshua	
Judges	
1 Samuel	
2 Samuel	
1 Kings	
2 Kings	
Ezra	
Nehemiah	

Joshua and Judges show the Hebrews entering Canaan, a land which God promised centuries earlier to give them. There they struggle with the tendency to turn away from the living God who loves and cares for them in order to turn to gods made by the hands of the Canaanites.

As time progresses the Hebrews transition from a confederation of twelve related tribes into a united kingdom ruled at various times by three different kings. First and 2 Samuel and part of 1 Kings tell of everything that happened during this time period of Old Testament history.

Unfortunately, a rebellion takes place splitting the kingdom into two separate countries, Israel in the north and Judah in the south. The last part of the book of 1 Kings and the beginning part of 2 Kings details all that happens during this time, including the country of Assyria conquering Israel.

Judah, however, does not remain free for long. Second Kings ends with Babylon taking Judah into exile. The captivity lasts about seventy years.

The books of Ezra and Nehemiah tell of God faithfully allowing the Hebrews to return to their promised land. There they wait for the coming Messiah which begins the New Testament.

TIME PERIOD	DESCRIPTION
Nothing Era	The human race out of nothing
Something Era	The Hebrew race into something
Exiting Era	Exiting Egypt
Entering Era	Entering Canaan
United Era	United kings stand
Divided Era	Divided kings fall
Scattered Era	Scattered Judah
Gathered Era	Gathered Judah

To help remember these eight time periods of Old Testament history, we will give each era a name. You find these in the previous chart. Notice that the names of the eight eras divide into four pairs of opposite words: **Nothing/Something, Exiting/Entering, United/Divided, and Scattered/ Gathered**. We have done this in order to make it easier to remember the eras. In the following chapters we will look more closely at each of these eras. Before we do, let's see how the other twenty-six books connect to these straight-edged pieces.

FILLING IN THE OTHER PIECES OF THE PUZZLE

The chart found on the following four pages takes the thirteen straight-edged puzzle pieces (think books) and appropriately divides them among the eight eras of Old Testament history. You will notice that lines connect some of the thirteen books to the other twenty-six books. A connection means that the events in each of the books occur during the same historical time frame. To go into detail about the additional twenty-six books falls outside the scope of our task. A brief summary of each one, however, can be found in appendix two at the end of this book.

Notice that we made some of the books different colors: black for the Historical Books, grey for the Poetical Books, and white for the Prophetical Books. For the most part, the Poetical Books occur during the United Era and the Prophetical Books are found throughout the Divided, Scattered, and Gathered Eras.

Take a moment now to examine how the other twenty-six Old Testament books fill in the border of the puzzle that the thirteen straight-edged pieces formed.

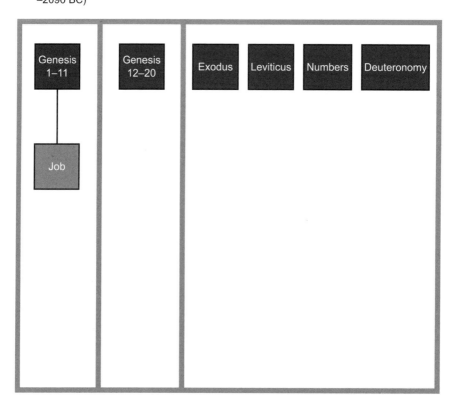

NOTHING
(CREATION
–2090 BC)

SOMETHING
(2090–1445 BC)

EXITING
(1445–1405 BC)

Genesis
1–11

Genesis
12–20

Exodus

Leviticus

Numbers

Deuteronomy

Job

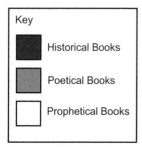

Key

Historical Books

Poetical Books

Prophetical Books

Old Testament

ENTERING
(1405–1043 BC)

UNITED
(1043–931 BC)

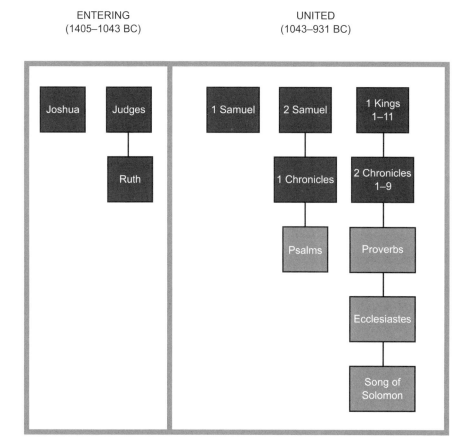

DIVIDED
(931–722/586 BC)

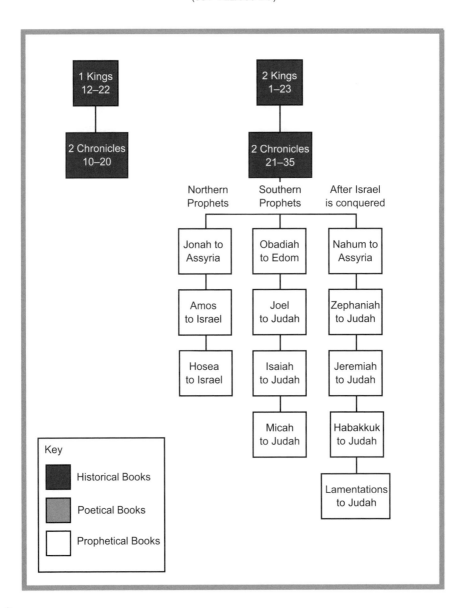

1 Kings
12–22

2 Chronicles
10–20

2 Kings
1–23

2 Chronicles
21–35

Northern Prophets	Southern Prophets	After Israel is conquered
Jonah to Assyria	Obadiah to Edom	Nahum to Assyria
Amos to Israel	Joel to Judah	Zephaniah to Judah
Hosea to Israel	Isaiah to Judah	Jeremiah to Judah
	Micah to Judah	Habakkuk to Judah
		Lamentations to Judah

Key

■ Historical Books

■ Poetical Books

□ Prophetical Books

Old Testament (continued)

SCATTERED
(605–538 BC)

GATHERED
(538 BC–CHRIST)

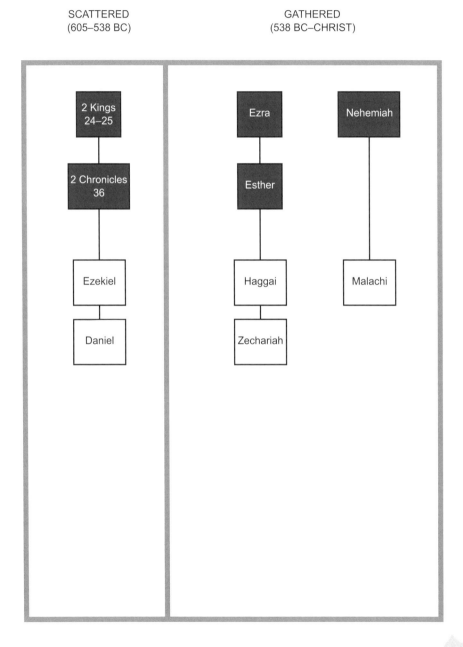

Now that we have the big picture of God receiving glory by restoring fellowship between all people groups and Himself through His Son, Jesus Christ, let's take a closer look at each of the eight eras. We will do this in such a way that, given just a little effort, will allow us to tell the story of what God did in preparing the nations for the coming Messiah.

FOR NEXT TIME

You may be working through this material with a group. If so, choose from one of the following options depending on how much preparation time you can devote this week.

Remember, you get out of something what you put into it. So the more time you can devote, the more you will learn. Yet, if there are weeks when life gets hectic and you can only do the bare minimum, don't feel guilty. These lessons are intended to motivate you as you seek to know God and His Word better.

	OPTION 1 "An extremely busy week"	OPTION 2 "A little extra time"	OPTION 3 "Can't get enough"
DO	Next chapter – Era 1	Next chapter – Era 1	Next chapter – Era 1
READ		Average Readers: Read Gen 1-3 about Adam and Eve Fast Readers: Add Gen 6-9 about Noah Speed Readers: Add Gen 4-5 and 10-11 about Cain and Abel and the Tower of Babel	Average Readers: Read Gen 1-3 about Adam and Eve Fast Readers: Add Gen 6-9 about Noah Speed Readers: Add Gen 4-5 and 10-11 about Cain and Abel and the Tower of Babel
MEMORIZE			Memorize the 39 books of the Old Testament

JUST FOR LAUGHS

A little girl became restless as the preacher's sermon dragged on and on. Finally, she leaned over to her mother and whispered, "Mommy, if we give him the money now, will he let us go?"

*   *   *

A boy was watching his father, a pastor, write a sermon. "How do you know what to say?" he asked. "I write down what God tells me." "Then why do you keep crossing things out?"

ERA #1

ERA #1

THE HUMAN RACE OUT OF NOTHING

(GENESIS 1-11)

As we saw in the introduction, the thirty-nine books of the Old Testament easily group into three different categories. Can you remember them? You can find the first category mentioned in the next paragraph, but if you look, some might call it cheating!

	Category	Number of Books
1.	_____	_____
2.	_____	_____
3.	_____	_____

The first seventeen books, called the Historical books, provide a timeline from creation until four hundred years before the time of Christ. We divided this timeline into eight eras. To help us better remember these eras we grouped them into four pairs of opposite words. Let's see how many you can remember. (If you need help getting started look back at the title at the beginning of this chapter.)

1. _____   5. _____

2. _____   6. _____

3. _____   7. _____

4. _____   8. _____

During this chapter we will take a closer look at the Nothing Era by answering six questions: what, how, where, when, who, and why. Let's begin by looking at the first of these—what was God doing during this period of biblical history?

WHAT?

During the Nothing Era, **God creates the human race**. Notice we did not say the Hebrew race. That's a big topic of the Bible and we will get to it in the next era, but it is not the main topic. If you recall the main topic of Scripture is God receiving glory by restoring fellowship between the human race and Himself through His Son, Jesus Christ. This first era describes how the human race came into being and why it needed to be brought back to God.

You may be wondering why we call it the Nothing Era. We call it the Nothing Era because that's exactly what God starts with when He sets out to make the human race. *Nothing!* No monkeys. No tadpoles. Not even a lump of clay. He just speaks and things start happening.

Well if that's what generally happens during this era, then how does it specifically happen?

HOW?

The Nothing Era contains **four events** directly related to the human race. First, God creates the heavens and earth crowning His work with the creation of man. Initially man is perfect and walks in unbroken fellowship with God. Unfortunately, the human race does not continue in this wonderful relationship, but disobeys God and falls out of fellowship with Him. As the corruption of man increases, God brings judgment on the human race destroying all but one man's family through the flood. Over time the human race once again forgets God and focuses on itself by building the tower of Babel. In response God confuses the language, dividing the human race into a variety of people groups. The following chart will help you better visualize where each of these events occurs in Scripture.

EVENT	SCRIPTURE	MAIN CHARACTERS
Creation	Genesis 1-2	God
Fall	Genesis 3-5	Adam and Eve
Flood	Genesis 6-9	Noah
Tower of Babel	Genesis 10-11	God

By the end of Genesis 11 the human race has begun to spread over the face of the earth and desperately needs to be brought back into a right relationship with God.

WHERE?

The Bible provides clear references as to where the fall, judgment, and division of man occur. They all are located in what's called the **Fertile Crescent**.

Genesis 2:10–14 describes the Garden of Eden, where Adam and Eve disobeyed God, placed between the Tigris and Euphrates Rivers. We know this area today (assuming the rivers have not changed courses dramatically) as the country of Iraq or maybe Syria and Turkey if Eden were further north. After the great flood Genesis 8:4 tells us that Noah's ark came to rest on the mountains of Ararat, located today in the modern country of Turkey. Genesis 11:2–4 mentions the Tower of Babel, where God confused man's language dividing the human race into its various cultures. They erected it on a plain in the land of Shinar. Shinar today is found in the country of Iraq. The maps below provide a general idea where each of these events took place. The first map uses Old Testament names of various landmarks. The

Sites Mentioned in Nothing Era

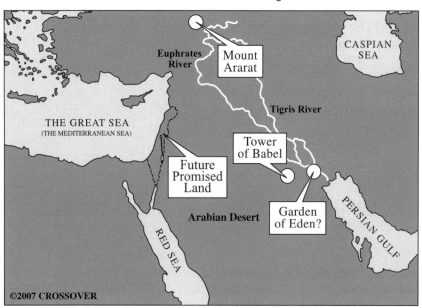

PUTTING TOGETHER THE PUZZLE OF THE OLD TESTAMENT

second map, however, may be more useful in orienting you to the general location of the events of this era since it shows the locations relative to the countries that exist in that part of the world today.

Today's Countries

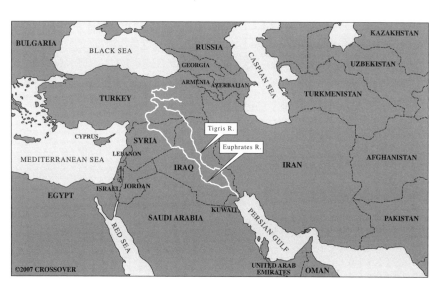

WHEN?

There are various positions for dating the beginning of creation. No one can state with absolute confidence as to exactly when everything all began. We can, however, be more precise at dating the close of this era since it is connected to a person named Abraham who we will meet in the next era. So we will date the Nothing Era as occurring from **Creation to 2090 BC**. The dating of subsequent eras will be much more precise.

WHO?

In this section and every other "Who?" section in the following chapters, we will pick one of the most famous characters of the era and see not only what we can learn *of* that person, but also what we can learn *from* that person.

The Nothing Era of the Old Testament is filled with some very well-known characters like Cain and Abel, as well as Noah and Mrs. Noah. It also contains others, mostly unknown to everyone except to the most studious of Bible scholars, people like Uz, Hul, Gether, and Mash, all grandsons of Shem who was the oldest son of Noah. But the most famous characters of this era are **Adam and Eve**.

By the end of the first two chapters of Genesis we find God has created Adam and Eve out of nothing and has placed them in the Garden of Eden. Everything is perfect. They are sinless, enabling them to live in intimate fellowship with God. As they rule over their domain, they only have one prohibition. What is it? Read Genesis 2:16–17 and write out the one thing they were not to do and why.

_____

_____

_____

Remember this: God gives us prohibitions, but never to penalize us. On the contrary, He does so in order to provide us with His best and to protect us from negative consequences. What "best" was God wanting to provide Adam and Eve; and from what consequence was He wanting to protect them?

_____

_____

_____

During Genesis 3 things go terribly wrong. The devil in the form of a serpent begins to tempt Eve to disobey God's one and only prohibition. Two observations should be noted about the way he goes about luring Eve away from God because he still uses the same strategy today. First, in Genesis 3:1–3 he subtly tempts Eve to question something that God has clearly communicated. Second, the devil twists God's words, minimizing the consequences and maximizing the perceived benefits of disobeying God's word.

Read Genesis 3:4–5 and note how the devil uses half-truths as he minimizes the consequences and maximizes the perceived benefits of God's words.

_____

_____

_____

What the devil sets in motion, the woman now carries to completion. She follows a pattern that many have copied after her. Read Genesis 3:6–7 and complete the following progression.

1. Eve saw the fruit.

2. Eve _____ the fruit.

3. Eve _____ the fruit.

4. Eve shared the fruit.

The disobedience of God's prohibition causes a break in fellowship with God. Adam and Eve know that they must now die. Seeking to forestall the inevitable, they try two hopeless tactics in Genesis 3:8–13. Initially they try to hide from God. This is impossible since God is present everywhere. Now cornered, Adam and Eve try their second trick, anything to get God's attention off of them. They try to put the blame on someone else. This, too, is ineffective because God is also omniscient, all-knowing, thus already aware of whose fault it really is. Read these verses and note who each of them blames.

_____

_____

_____

The ultimate negative consequence from which God had sought to protect Adam and Eve occurs immediately. They die and, as a result, the rest of the future human race dies as well. Scripture uses the word "die" in two different ways: to die physically and to die spiritually (see Ephesians 2:1). Physical death separates one from the earth. Spiritual death separates one from God.

Read Genesis 3:23–24 and Genesis 5:5. In what ways did Adam and Eve die and which occurred first?

_____

_____

_____

So what have we learned from Adam and Eve?

Lesson 1 – Whenever God gives a command it is to provide us with benefits and to protect us from consequences.

Lesson 2 – The devil entices us to disobey God by maximizing the benefits of sin and minimizing the consequences of sin.

Lesson 3 – Our sin tends to follow this pattern: it starts in our head, moves to our heart, and ends with our hands.

> **temptation**: The desire to fulfill a God-given drive in a God-forbidden way.

Lesson 4 – There are two wrong ways to handle disobedience: hiding from God and blaming our wrong-doing on others. (In the "Who?" section of the fifth Old Testament era, we learn the correct way to deal with our disobedience.)

Lesson 5 – Adam and Eve's original sin broke fellowship with God and brought us death, both physical and spiritual death.

With these and perhaps other lessons in mind, what specifically from Adam and Eve can you apply to your life so you can have closer fellowship with God?

_____

_____

_____

Second Corinthians 11:3 says, "But I am afraid, as the serpent deceived Eve by his craftiness, your minds will be led astray from the simplicity and purity of devotion to Christ." May we be alert to the craftiness of the devil so we can stay devoted to Christ and thus walk in intimate fellowship with God.

You do not need to fill in the following chart. This summary chart will be filled in for you after each "Who?" section in the subsequent chapters.

FOUR AREAS OF SPIRITUAL GROWTH	IMPROPER STEPS	PROPER STEPS
Fellowship with God	Era 1 – Hiding our sin from God or blaming it on others.	Era 5 –
Trust in God	Era 2 –	Era 6 –
Obedience to God	Era 3 –	Era 7 –
Hearing from God	Era 4 –	Era 8 –

WHY?

One often hears that the most important aspect about anything is its purpose. So what is the purpose of the Nothing Era? Remember the main topic of the Bible is God receiving glory by restoring fellowship between the human race and Himself through His Son, Jesus Christ. This era of the Bible explains God's purpose for man (fellowship with Him for eternity) and God's problem with man (fellowship broken because of man's disobedience). This era of Scripture also communicates God's solution for man—God would provide a Messiah to save man from the consequences of his disobedience. It surprises most people to learn this era introduces not only God and man, but Jesus Christ as well. (Note: The third person of the Trinity, the Holy Spirit, is also introduced in the Nothing Era. Check out Genesis 1:2.)

You may be thinking, "Whoa! Genesis 1–11 never mentions Jesus Christ." But it does, though admittedly not specifically. That's why most people miss it. He's introduced in Genesis 3:15 when God rebukes Satan who has taken the form of a snake. God says, "And I will put enmity between you and the woman, and between your seed and her seed; he shall bruise you on the head, and you shall bruise him on the heel."

This verse speaks of two future events: Satan bruising the heel of mankind and the seed of woman crushing the head of Satan. The seed of woman refers to Jesus Christ who would one day come to **overcome the works of the devil**. First John 3:8 says, "The Son of God appeared for this purpose, to destroy the works of the devil."

Please don't allow the vagueness of Genesis 3:15 to frustrate you. Be patient. We will find that as Scripture progresses through the various eras, the coming of Christ becomes more clearly revealed. So clearly in fact that by the eighth and final era of the Old Testament, which ends hundreds of years before the coming of Christ, God's people know the exact time and place of His future appearing!

A LITTLE EXTRA

The first six days of creation divide into three pairs. Each pair consists of a realm and a corresponding ruler. On the seventh day of creation, God rested.

THE SEVEN DAYS OF CREATION

DAY	REALM	DAY	RULER
1	Light (Gen 1:3-5)	4	Sun, moon, and stars (Gen 1:14-19)
2	Heaven and water (Gen 1:6-8)	5	Birds and fish (Gen 1:20-23)
3	Earth (Gen 1:9-13)	6	Animals and people (Gen 1:24-31)
7	God rested (Gen 2:1-3)		

FOR NEXT TIME

	OPTION 1 "An extremely busy week"	OPTION 2 "A little extra time"	OPTION 3 "Can't get enough"
DO	Next chapter – Era 2	Next chapter – Era 2	Next chapter – Era 2
READ		Average Readers: Read Gen 12-24 about Abraham Fast Readers: Add Gen 37-50 about Joseph Speed Readers: Add Gen 25-26 and 27-36 about Isaac and Jacob	Average Readers: Read Gen 12-24 about Abraham Fast Readers: Add Gen 37-50 about Joseph Speed Readers: Add Gen 25-26 and 27-36 about Isaac and Jacob
MEMORIZE** (CHOOSE ONE)			Nothing Era verse: Genesis 1:27 First application verse: Genesis 3:6 First Christ verse: Genesis 3:15 First personal verse: choose your own

** Each week you can memorize one (or all!) of the four verses. The Era verses will help you remember the eight historical eras of the Old Testament. The application verses will encourage your own spiritual growth. The Christ verses will provide you with an understanding of where scripture mentions the coming Messiah. The personal verses allow you to memorize any verse that you discovered in your reading that meant a great deal to you.

JUST FOR LAUGHS***

Little Johnny opened the huge family Bible and with fascination looked at each of the ancient pages. As he turned them one by one, an old tree leaf that had been pressed in between the pages fell out. Picking it up he examined it closely until he was convinced of what he had found. Astonished, he cried out to his mom, "Look what I found! It's a pair of Adam's pants!"

* * *

A Sunday school teacher asked little Johnny, "Do you think Noah did a lot of fishing when he was on the ark?" He replied, "Of course not. How could he? Noah only had two worms."

* * *

The teacher explained to little Johnny's Sunday school class how God had created Eve from one of Adam's ribs. Later that week Johnny's mother noticed him lying down with a painful expression on his face. When she asked what was wrong, he responded, "I have a pain in my side. I think God is making me a wife."

* * *

The following unedited statements come from the writings of elementary school students. Pay particular attention to the spelling.

In the first book of the Bible, Guinessis, God got tired of creating the world so He took the Sabbath off.

The first commandment was when Eve told Adam to eat the apple.

Adam and Eve were created from a apple tree. Noah's wife was Joan of Ark. Noah built an ark and the animals came on in rears.

* * *

A little girl was sitting on her grandfather's lap as he read her a bedtime story. From time to time, she would take her eyes off the book and reach up to touch his wrinkled cheek. She was alternately stroking her own cheek, then his again. Finally she spoke up, "Grandpa, did God make you?" He answered, "Yes, sweetheart, God made me a long time ago." "Oh." Then after a long pause she asked, "Grandpa, did God make me too?" "Yes, indeed, God made you just a little while ago." Feeling their respective faces again, she observed, "God's getting better at it, isn't He?"

*** All jokes in the Just for Laughs sections were found on the Internet and appear to be in public domain.

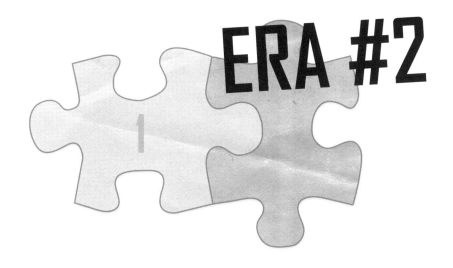

ERA #2

ERA #2

THE HEBREW RACE INTO SOMETHING

(GENESIS 12-50)

Before learning about the Something Era, let's see how much you remember about the Nothing Era. Without looking back at the last chapter, see how many blanks of the following chart you can complete. In the first column list the four key events that took place during Era #1 and in the last column note the names of the main characters.

EVENT	SCRIPTURE	MAIN CHARACTERS
	Genesis 1-2	
	Genesis 3-5	_____ and _____
	Genesis 6-9	
	Genesis 10-11	God

In Era #1 we discovered how God created the human race out of nothing. The first people, Adam and Eve, walked in unbroken fellowship with God because He had created them morally perfect. Unfortunately, that privileged experience did not last very long. Adam and Eve disobeyed God causing a huge separation between them and their creator.

This sad event provides the context for the whole Bible. God loves the human race so much He sets in motion a plan so glorious it would be unbelievable if God Himself were not the author. God proclaims He will send through the woman, Eve, an offspring who would one day overcome the damaging effects caused by the serpent. The rest of Scripture elaborates on this theme: God receiving glory by restoring fellowship between the human race and Himself through His Son, Jesus Christ.

Do you remember which verse in Genesis 3 prophesies the coming Christ? _____

By the end of the Nothing Era, God has divided the human race into different ethnic or people groups by confusing their languages. The next question should be obvious. From which of these cultural groups would the promised Deliverer come? Let's focus now on the Something Era found in Genesis 12–50 and discover which people group becomes the chosen nation.

WHAT?

During this second era we find God **choosing the Hebrew race** and turning it into something. The word "something" contains two meanings. The first refers to the significance of the Hebrews and the second to their size. In a moment you will see why we can appropriately apply both to the Hebrew people.

The Something Era begins in Genesis 12. There in the very first verse we find God speaking to a man named Abraham. (Actually at that point his name is Abram, but God later renames him Abraham.) In three short verses,

Genesis 12:1–3, we make two big discoveries. First we find what Abraham will do for God. God tells Abraham to leave his homeland and go to a new country. Abraham obeys and God leads him to the land of Canaan. Second we learn what God will do for Abraham. God promises to make Abraham into a great nation. True to His promise, God eventually turns the offspring of Abraham into the Hebrew nation.

Well, what is the significance of this Hebrew nation? In these same three verses God tells Abraham that in him all the families of the earth will be blessed. God blesses Abraham so that he will be a blessing. We will look more deeply at this later in the "Why?" section.

And the size? By the end of the second era, Scripture describes the Hebrew race this way, "But the sons of Israel were fruitful and increased greatly, and multiplied, and became exceedingly mighty, so that the land was filled with them" (Exodus 1:7). So how did they grow to such a great number?

HOW?

The Hebrew race did not become a great nation very quickly. It took almost two hundred years before they even numbered in triple digits. The slow growth rate resulted from a very specific reason. During the Something Era, the first Hebrew men kept marrying barren women.

Abraham set the precedent. His wife, Sarah, could not bear children. How was God going to make him into a great nation if Sarah could not even produce the first child? A barren womb, however, presents no huge obstacle to God. If He created the human race out of nothing, then certainly He could do the same for the Hebrew race. And He did. Abraham and Sarah in their old age give birth to Isaac.

When Isaac grows into manhood, he marries Rebekah, but the same problem exists. Rebekah also is barren. In answer to prayer God gives them twins, Jacob and Esau. Years later when Jacob marries, his wife Rachel is, you guessed it, also barren. Yet God, faithful to His promise, eventually gives Jacob twelve sons though not all by Rachel. The descendents of these twelve become the twelve tribes of Israel, another name for Jacob, which make up the Hebrew nation.

One of Jacob's twelve sons was Joseph. Out of jealousy his brothers sell him into slavery. Through an unusual series of circumstances, he rises from the status of a slave to occupy the second most powerful position in Egypt, second only to the Pharaoh himself. From this position he saves the Hebrews from starvation during a famine in the land of Canaan by inviting them to Egypt where he cares for them. There in Egypt they grow into a great multitude.

SCRIPTURE	MAIN CHARACTERS
Genesis 12-24	Abraham
Genesis 25-26	Isaac
Genesis 27-36	Jacob
Genesis 37-50	Joseph

The fascinating stories of these first **four patriarchs**, or fathers, detail the fulfillment of God's promise to turn Abraham's offspring into something—a great nation in both size and significance.

Let's look at where and when this era of the Old Testament occurred.

WHERE?

This second era of Old Testament history covers a lot of geography. It starts with Abraham leaving Ur which is in the modern country of Iraq. It ends with Joseph and his brothers in Egypt. In between these two places, most of the events occur in **the land of Canaan** which is the modern country of Israel with parts of Syria, Lebanon, and Jordan. It is this area God promises to give to Abraham's descendants.

Abraham's Journeys

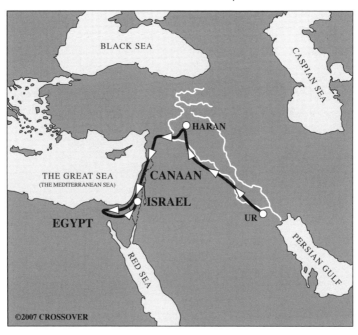

Joseph's Journey to Egypt

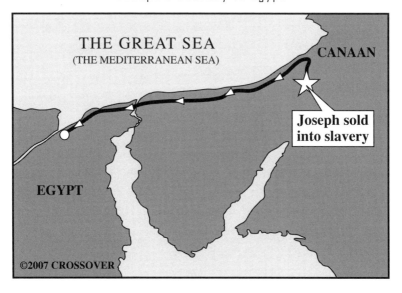

WHEN?

We can date the Something Era far more accurately than we dated the Nothing Era. Most scholars put the death of Abraham's father (Genesis 11:32) which ends the first era and begins the second era at approximately 2090 BC. The end of the Something Era ends with the exodus of the Hebrews from Egypt which falls around 1445 BC. So the Something Era lasts approximately 645 years between **2090–1445 BC**.

ERA	Nothing	Something
GENESIS	Chapters 1-11	Chapters 12-50
WHAT?	Human race	Hebrew race
HOW?	Four events:	Four patriarchs:
	Creation	*Abraham*
	Fall	*Isaac*
	Flood	*Jacob*
	Tower of Babel	*Joseph*
WHERE?	Fertile Crescent	Promised Canaan
WHEN?	Thousands of years	Hundreds of years

The book of Genesis begins with the Nothing Era and ends with the Something Era. The above chart makes the content of this book easy to remember.

WHO?

Of the four patriarchs from whom we could choose, it seems appropriate that we pick **Abraham** to examine more closely since three world-wide religions look to him as the father of their faith: Christians, Jews and Muslims. What then can we learn from Abraham? We could learn many spiritual truths, but let's focus on his faith.

We learned in the "What?" and "How?" sections above that God promised to turn Abraham's descendents into a great nation even though his wife, Sarah, could not bear children. As they both advanced in age, you would think that Abraham would lose his faith in God's ability to fulfill his promise. Yet he doesn't. Romans 4:19–21 describes Abraham's faith. Write these verses in your own words.

_____

_____

_____

Finally at age 89, the patriarch's wife conceives and nine months later gives birth to Isaac. Could a man ever experience a greater test of his faith in God? Most definitely. In Genesis 22, God puts Abraham's faith to the ultimate test.

By Genesis 22, about thirty-five to forty years after God's promise of a descendant, Abraham now has a young son whom he dearly loves. In the first two verses of this chapter, however, God makes a very confusing request. He asks Abraham to offer Isaac as a sacrifice on a mountain in the land of Moriah.

In verses 3–5 we find Abraham making preparations and then traveling to the land of Moriah with Isaac and two servants. On the third day he arrives and leaves the two men to offer Isaac as a sacrifice. Before he leaves, he makes a statement in verse 5 to his servants that provides great insight into Abraham's faith and perhaps answers why it does not appear he argued with God about offering his beloved son. Can you find it? What does he say?

_____

_____

If you didn't catch it, that's okay since the insight comes from only two letters. He tells the men that "we" will return, not "I" will return. For him and Isaac to return would mean one of at least three options would have to be true. First, Abraham never intended to sacrifice his son. Second, Abraham believed God would provide a substitute. Or third, Abraham believed if he sacrificed Isaac that God would raise his son from the dead. The next three verses give part of the answer. (You will find the rest of the answer in Hebrews 11:17–19.)

As they walk to the place of sacrifice in verses 6–8, Isaac asks his father a very logical question, "Behold, the fire and the wood, but where is the lamb for the burnt offering?" Abraham answers his son in verse 8. From what Abraham says, which of the above options do you think he had in mind and why?

_____

_____

_____

Whether Abraham had to force his son to become a potential offering, we don't know. Yet we can confidently assume the following experience would leave a powerful image in Isaac's memory and would serve to strengthen his own faith in the future. In verses 9–10 we find Isaac lying on a stack of wood with his hands tied and his father reaching for a knife. Abraham had been trusting God to provide a sacrifice, yet from Abraham's perspective, time has expired and he sees no substitute. Fear is the opposite of faith. Do you think fear attacked Abraham at this point? Why or why not?

_____

_____

_____

Just in time, in verses 11–14, an angel stops Abraham from killing his son by showing him a ram caught by the horns in a nearby thicket. Abraham offers the ram as the substitute for his son and calls this mountain in the land of Moriah "The Lord Will Provide." Most scholars believe that the mountain on which Abraham offered Isaac is the same mountain on which Solomon would later build the temple in the future city of Jerusalem, the city where God later offers His own Son as a sacrifice for mankind's sin.

In verses 15–18 the angel speaks to Abraham a second time. What does the angel say and what impact do you think this has on Abraham's faith?

_____

_____

_____

In the last verse of this passage, verse 19, we find Abraham and Isaac returning to the young men just as he believed he would and with having seen God provide as he believed He would.

What lessons can we learn from Abraham?

Lesson 1 – We can have faith in what God tells us because God is faithful. That's part of who He is.

Lesson 2 – A person's faith in God can grow. So if you find yourself with little faith in what God tells you, there is hope. Your faith can grow to the limit of God's faithfulness.

Lesson 3 – You grow your faith when you trust God to do what He said He would do. Think in terms of exercising a muscle. The more you use it, the stronger it becomes.

Lesson 4 – Sometimes God waits a long time (from our perspective) to do what He said He would do. So be patient.

Lesson 5 – The opposite of faith is fear, so if you find yourself fearful, you have the wrong focus. Immediately place it back where it belongs, on God and His faithfulness.

From these and other insights you gained from reading about this second historical era of the Old Testament, what can you apply to your own life to grow in your faith?

_____

_____

_____

Hebrews 11:17–19 says, "By faith Abraham, when he was tested, offered up Isaac, and he who had received the promises was offering up his only begotten son; it was he to whom it was said, 'In Isaac your descendants shall be called.' He considered that God is able to raise people even from the dead; from which he also received him back as a type." May Abraham's faith encourage you to trust more fully the faithfulness of God. We can now add to our summary chart of ways we can mature in our spiritual journey.

FOUR AREAS OF SPIRITUAL GROWTH	IMPROPER STEPS	PROPER STEPS
Fellowship with God	Era 1 – Hiding our sin from God or blaming it on others.	Era 5 –
Trust in God	Era 2 – Allowing fear to paralyze us.	Era 6 –
Obedience to God	Era 3 –	Era 7 –
Hearing from God	Era 4 –	Era 8 –

WHY?

If you remember in the "What?" section we discovered the significance of the Hebrew nation from Genesis 12:2–3. In this passage God told Abraham,

"And I will make you a great nation, and I will bless you, and make your name great; and so you shall be a blessing . . . And in you all the families of the earth shall be blessed." Let's divide these verses into three parts:

- God's promise for His people: I will bless you.

- God's plan for His people: So you shall be a blessing.

- God's purpose for His people: In you all the families of the earth shall be blessed.

God promised in these verses that He would bless Abraham and turn the Hebrew people into something, a great nation. Though that was not the end of God's proclamation, unfortunately it became the only focus of Abraham's descendants. Life centered completely on themselves. That always happens when a person or group of persons confuses God's promise for His plan.

God's plan was for His people to focus not on themselves, but on others. They were to be a blessing. He promised to bless them SO THAT they would be a blessing. But they forgot the "so that." They fixated on God's *promise* (being blessed by God) and as a result ignored God's *plan* (being a blessing for God).

But what can we discover about God's purpose in all of this? As these verses continue, God tells Abraham that in him all the families of the earth will be blessed. "In him" refers to Abraham's seed or offspring. (Also see Genesis 22:18.) "All the families of the earth" or as some Bibles put it "all the nations of the earth" refers to ethnic or people groups. (Remember, nations did not exist back then as we know them today. So don't think countries, think cultures.) Simply put, this passage adds to what we learned about Jesus Christ from the Nothing Era. There we learned that Christ was coming to overcome the works of the serpent. During the Something Era we learn from which nation He would come. This second era **shows Christ coming from the seed of Abraham**. Galatians 3:16 confirms this truth. "Now the promises were spoken to Abraham and to his seed. He does not say, 'And to seeds,' as referring to many, but rather to one, 'And to your seed,' that is, Christ.

This passage of Scripture also reinforces another lesson we learned during the Nothing Era. There we discovered God's heart was for the human race. We see it here also when Genesis 12 refers to "all the families of the earth." Many people have the misconception that God's heart in the Old Testament was only for the Hebrew race. They mistakenly believe that it was not until the New Testament that God turned His heart to the human race. Not true! God's heart from the beginning of the Bible to its end has always been for the human race. The book of Galatians once again confirms this. Chapter three, verse eight says, "And the Scripture foreseeing that God would justify the Gentiles by faith, preached the gospel beforehand to Abraham, saying 'All the nations shall be blessed in you.'"

What a powerful passage! God blessed the Hebrews SO THAT they would be a blessing to all the other people groups of the world by announcing that a Deliverer was coming to overcome sin and Satan.

A LITTLE EXTRA

People sometimes get confused when they compare the twelve sons of Israel (Jacob) in Genesis 29–30 with maps like the one in this book in the "Why" section of the Entering Era on page 84 that shows the location of the twelve tribes of Israel once they enter the Promised Land of Canaan. The map does not show Israel's third son, Levi, or eleventh son, Joseph, receiving any land.

THE TWELVE TRIBES OF ISRAEL (OR WAS IT THIRTEEN?)

12 SONS OF ISRAEL	12 TRIBES OF ISRAEL
Reuben	Reuben
Simeon	Simeon
Levi	Levi (priests)
Judah	Judah
Dan	Dan
Naphtali	Naphtali
Gad	Gad

Asher	Asher
Issachar	Issachar
Zebulun	Zebulun
Joseph	Ephraim and Manasseh
Benjamin	Benjamin
12 sons	13 tribes, 12 with land

The tribe of Levi received no portion of the Promised Land because they inherited something far better. Deuteronomy 18:2 says of the Levites, "They shall have no inheritance among their countrymen; the LORD is their inheritance, as He promised them." God made the Levites a tribe of priests and dispersed them throughout the other tribes so they could continually remind the others of God's presence.

The tribe of Joseph does not exist because when Jacob blessed Joseph in Genesis 48, he made Joseph's two oldest children his own. The descendants of these two sons became the tribes of Ephraim and Manasseh and received portions of the Promised Land.

FOR NEXT TIME

	OPTION 1 "An extremely busy week"	OPTION 2 "A little extra time"	OPTION 3 "Can't get enough"
DO	Next chapter – Era 3	Next chapter – Era 3	Next chapter – Era 3

READ		Average Readers: Read Exodus 5-18 about the plagues Fast Readers: Add Exodus 1-4 about Moses Speed Readers: Add Exodus 19-40 about the 10 Commandments and the tabernacle	Average Readers: Read Exodus 5-18 about the plagues Fast Readers: Add Exodus 1-4 about Moses Speed Readers: Add Exodus 19-40 about the 10 Commandments and the tabernacle
MEMORIZE (Choose one)			Second Era verse: Exodus 1:7 Second application verse: Genesis 22:14 Second Christ verse: Genesis 12:2-3 Second personal verse: choose your own

JUST FOR LAUGHS

One morning the Sunday school teacher taught about Lot, Abraham's nephew, escaping from Sodom and Gomorrah. As she described how Lot's wife looked back and turned into a pillar of salt, little Johnny interrupted, "My mommy looked back once, while she was driving," announcing triumphantly, "and she turned into a telephone pole!"

ERA #3

ERA #3

EXITING EGYPT

(EXODUS—DEUTERONOMY)

Review time! In the chart below, fill in the four key events that occurred during Era #1 and the names of the four patriarchs on whom Era #2 focused. Please answer as much as possible without looking back at the previous two chapters. Also, at the top of the chart, fill in the missing key words for each of these Old Testament historical eras.

ERA #1 THE HUMAN RACE OUT OF _____	ERA #2 THE HEBREW RACE INTO _____

In the last chapter we discovered that God chose the Hebrew race in order to bless them. The Lord promised Abraham and his descendants that they would one day inhabit a land as a great nation. Yet this blessing was not an end to itself. God blessed them SO THAT they would be a blessing by announcing to the nations the coming Messiah who would overcome the consequences caused by Adam and Eve's disobedience to God's command.

Do you remember the Scripture reference where God pronounced to Abraham this incredible blessing of the coming Messiah? _____

In spite of several barren wombs, by the close of the second era, God turns the Hebrew race into something, a people of great size and significance. But now a new set of problems exist. If you remember, Joseph invites Jacob and his family to move to Egypt because of famine. Four hundred and thirty years later, however, they still live in Egypt and not in Canaan, the land which God had promised them. To complicate matters the Egyptians have enslaved God's people to build cities for the pharaohs.

God, however, was about to change all that.

WHAT?

Think about it. Everything that occurred in the previous two eras took place in the very first book of the Bible, Genesis. The third era of Old Testament history, however, covers four books of the Bible: Exodus, Leviticus, Numbers, and Deuteronomy. As you can imagine, that's a lot of information. Fortunately we can summarize the theme of the Exiting Era very easily. During this time, God focuses on **delivering the Hebrews from Egypt**.

Yet what hope did the Hebrews have for deliverance from their bondage? For centuries the Egyptian economy has depended on its plentiful source of cheap labor. No government would readily release from their grip such an extremely valuable national resource. A Hebrew rebellion seemed foolish since the most powerful country on earth enslaved them. They realize it would require God Himself to set them free. At the beginning of this third era we find the Hebrews crying out for the God of Abraham, Isaac, Jacob, and Joseph to deliver them.

So how does He do this and how can we remember it?

HOW?

As mentioned earlier, the content of Exodus, Leviticus, Numbers, and Deuteronomy record the history of the Exiting Era. Interestingly, the **four titles** of these books tell the story of how God delivers His people, but you need to know what the titles mean.

The title "Exodus" means departure. The title "Leviticus" means pertaining to the Levites, more specifically to the Levitical priests. "Numbers" refers to counting and the title of "Deuteronomy" results from combining the Greek words for second (deuteron) and law (nomon).

TITLE	MEANING
Exodus	Departing from/to a place
Leviticus	Relating to the Levitical priests
Numbers	Counting of numbers
Deuteronomy	Referring to the second law

Now let's see how these titles tell the story of God delivering His people.

During the book of Exodus, the departure contains three aspects: from Egypt, through the Red Sea, and to Mount Sinai. First, God calls Moses to challenge Pharaoh to release the Hebrews. When Pharaoh refuses Moses' request, God sends ten plagues upon the Egyptians. The last plague takes the life of all the first-born, sparing only those who had applied the blood of a special "Passover" lamb to the doorway of their home. Because of the devastation caused by this final plague, Pharaoh relents and the Hebrews *depart from* Egypt. Soon afterward Pharaoh sends an army to bring them back to him. God parts the waters allowing the Hebrews to *depart through* the Red

Sea. Safely on the other side of the sea, the Hebrews watch as God closes the waters destroying the pursuing Egyptian army. From there the Hebrews *depart to* Mount Sinai where God gives them the Ten Commandments.

The title "Leviticus" pertains to the duties of the Levitical priests. While at Mount Sinai, God prepares his people to worship Him in the newly constructed tabernacle (a place of worship) by instituting five different types of offerings and seven different annual feasts. Each offering and feast contains significant historical and spiritual meaning.

FIVE OFFERINGS	SEVEN FEASTS
Burnt (Leviticus 1)	Passover (Leviticus 23:4-5)
Meal (Leviticus 2)	Unleavened Bread (Leviticus 23:6-8)
Peace (Leviticus 3)	First Fruits (Leviticus 23:9-14)
Sin (Leviticus 4)	Pentecost (Leviticus 23:15-22)
Grain (Leviticus 5)	Trumpets (Leviticus 23:23-25)
	Atonement (Leviticus 23:26-32)
	Tabernacles (Leviticus 23:33-44)

The third book bears the title "Numbers" because in this book Moses twice numbers the population of his people. The first census takes place while still at Mount Sinai. After tallying the number, the Hebrews begin their journey to Canaan. After centuries of waiting, now only days separate them from their Promised Land. Unfortunately, after spying out the land at Kadesh, the Hebrews decide the people who inhabit the land will destroy them. They refuse to believe the God who delivered them from the most feared fighting force on the planet could deliver them from the various people groups who lived in Canaan. As a result God disciplines them by making them wander in the wilderness (Numbers 33:1–49 records their itinerary) until the entire disbelieving generation passes away. At the end of the book, Moses counts a new generation of Hebrews in preparation once again to enter the Promised Land and divide it among the twelve tribes of Israel. The larger tribes will receive a larger allotment of the land and the smaller tribes will receive a smaller allotment of the land (Numbers 26:2, 54).

	1-13	The Hebrews depart from Egypt after the ten plagues
EXODUS	13-18	The Hebrews depart through the Red Sea escaping from Pharaoh's army
	19-40	The Hebrews depart to Mount Sinai where they (1st generation) receive the Ten Commandments
LEVITICUS	1-27	Moses instructs the Levitical priests regarding five offerings and seven feasts
	1-12	Moses counts the Hebrews who lived in Egypt (1st generation)
	13-19	At Kadesh the Hebrews refuse to enter the Promised Land
NUMBERS	20-25	The Hebrews wander for almost forty years in the wilderness
	26-36	Moses counts the Hebrews who will live in the Promised Land (2nd generation)
DEUTERONOMY	1-34	Moses reviews the Ten Commandments (2nd generation)

The fourth title "Deuteronomy" reminds us of what occurs next during the Exiting Era. In this book Moses prepares a new generation of Hebrews for the Promised Land. The previous generation who had heard the Ten Commandments when God initially gave them at Mount Sinai had now died while wandering in the wilderness. To ready the new generation for entering the Promised Land, Moses reminds them of what God considers most important by reviewing the Ten Commandments. With this second formal giving of the Ten Commandments, the Hebrews stand ready to enter the Promised Land, but that's for the next chapter.

WHERE?

The Exiting Era starts in **Egypt** and, as we have found, ends at the doorway to the Promised Land. The Hebrews, however, covered a lot of unnecessary ground in between these two points. To help remember the most important sites during this era, the chart below connects each title with its key geographical locations.

EXODUS	Traveling from Egypt to Mount Sinai
LEVITICUS	Standing still at Mount Sinai
NUMBERS	Traveling from Mount Sinai to Kadesh and then through the Wilderness to Moab
DEUTERONOMY	Standing still at Moab

The location of these key places can be found on the map below.

Traditional Route of the Exodus

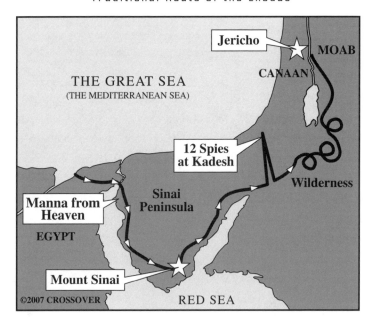

The wandering of the people of God ends in Moab, located to the east of Jericho where Moses dies without ever stepping foot into the Promised Land. The Lord does, however, allow him to view the land from the top of Mount Nebo, a mountain rising above the plains of Moab. (Read Deuteronomy 34:1-8.)

WHEN?

Moses lived from 1525 to 1405 BC. The Exiting Era occurs during the last forty years of his life (Ex 7:7 and Deu 34:7), placing this third era between **1445 and 1405 BC**. The four books of this era divide these forty years as follows:

EXODUS	1 year (starting with the Passover in Ex 12)
LEVITICUS	1 month
NUMBERS	Almost 39 years
DEUTERONOMY	1 month

WHO?

Throughout each of the four books written during the Exiting Era, **Moses** stands out as the main character. In the book of Exodus, he delivers his people from Egypt, parts the Red Sea with his staff, and receives the Ten Commandments from God at Mount Sinai. During Leviticus, he instructs the priests about their duties. He guides the people of Israel as they wander in the wildness as recorded by the book of Numbers. And he prepares the new generation in the book of Deuteronomy to enter the Promised Land. What then can we learn from this great man of God?

Many passages within these four books offer tremendous insight into how we can grow spiritually, but one stands out—Exodus 32. This chapter deals with the episode of the golden calf. Before we look more closely at this low point in the history of Israel, let's recall the context.

God, in Exodus 20:1–18, gives Moses and the Hebrews the Ten Commandments at Mount Sinai amidst much thunder, lightning, and smoke. This frightens the people. Who would not be scared? Why do you think God made such a big display?

_____

_____

_____

In verses 19–21 while assuring the people, Moses makes an interesting comment about God's reason for doing this. What is it?

_____

_____

_____

In verses 22–23 God speaks again. Now keep in mind, these words follow immediately after giving the Ten Commandments. Notice that God repeats one of the Ten Commandments. Which one? Why do you think He repeated this particular commandment and not one of the others?

_____

_____

Let's look at one other verse before we get to the story of the golden calf. Read Exodus 24:7. What are the very last words the people say to Moses before he leaves for Mount Sinai again? Write them in capital letters.

_____

_____

_____

Now let's look at chapter 32 of Exodus. As the chapter begins, we find Moses on Mount Sinai receiving the Ten Commandments on two stone tablets. This trip, however, lasts longer than the other three. He is gone forty days and forty nights. Read verse one. When Moses delays in returning, the people ask Aaron (the priest who had been by Moses' side since the first plague) for something. What is it and what do you think motivated them to want it, especially after all they recently had experienced?

_____

_____

_____

Read verses 2–6. What does Aaron do? Does this surprise you?

_____

_____

_____

As this scene unfolds, God tells Moses in verses 7–18 that he must return to the people because of what they have done. Read verses 19–20. How does Moses respond when he sees the people of God worshipping a golden calf?

_____

_____

_____

In the next four verses Moses confronts Aaron. How does Aaron respond and which character from the Nothing Era does he remind you of? Make sure you read verse 24 carefully.

_____

_____

_____

Verses 25–35 record God's response to their disobedience. What does God do? Do you think His discipline was appropriate? Why? Do you think the people saw this coming?

_____

_____

_____

What lessons on obedience can we learn from Moses' encounter with the golden calf?

Lesson 1 – Obedience, as much as anything, shows God that we love Him. (Check out John 14:21.)

Lesson 2 – God is a jealous God and does not want anything, not anything, to come between Him and us. (See Exodus 20:5.)

Lesson 3 – When we disobey God, He disciplines us to win us back, not to pay us back. (See Hebrews 12:5–11.)

Lesson 4 – You can choose your sin, but you cannot choose the consequences of your sin. (Notice Exodus 32:35.)

What other lessons can you add from this week's lesson or reading?

_____

_____

_____

Which of these lessons will you apply to your life?

_____

_____

_____

First Peter 1:14–16 says, "As obedient children, do not be conformed to the former lusts which were yours in your ignorance, but like the Holy One who called you, be holy yourselves also in all your behavior; because it is written, 'You shall be holy, for I am holy.'" May the example of Moses and the golden calf motivate us to walk more obediently as God's children. Now let's add to our spiritual growth chart.

FOUR AREAS OF SPIRITUAL GROWTH	IMPROPER STEPS	PROPER STEPS
Fellowship with God	Era 1 – Hiding our sin from God or blaming it on others.	Era 5 –
Trust in God	Era 2 – Allowing fear to paralyze us.	Era 6 –
Obedience to God	Era 3 – Failing to follow-through on what God has commanded us to do.	Era 7 –
Hearing from God	Era 4 –	Era 8 –

WHY?

The previous two eras revealed that a messiah, we know Him as Jesus Christ, would one day come from a descendant of Abraham to overcome the serpent and the consequences of man's sin. God would send this messiah, not just for the Hebrew race, but for the human race. God had chosen to bless them SO THAT they would a blessing to all the peoples of the earth. The Old Testament contains many pictures or types that point toward this coming One. In this era, **the Passover Lamb serves as a powerful picture of Christ.** Let's see why.

If you remember, the last plague God brought upon Egypt concerned the death of every first-born. For the Hebrews to avoid plague, the Lord instructed through Moses in Exodus 12 for each family after caring for an unblemished lamb to kill it, putting the blood on the doorway of the house. The people were then to eat the lamb served with unleavened bread. In so doing, God would spare them from His judgment. The very next year this practice became an annual feast which the Hebrews celebrated to remind them that God had delivered them from their bondage. During future sacrifices the priests poured the blood of the Passover lamb upon the altar of the tabernacle and ultimately the temple instead of applying the blood to a doorway. The Passover Lamb serves as a picture of the coming Christ in several ways as the next chart demonstrates.

PASSOVER		CHRIST	
Lamb	Exodus 12:3	"Behold, the Lamb of God who takes away the sin of the world."	John 1:29
Unblemished	Exodus 12:5	"As of a lamb unblemished and spotless, the blood of Christ . . ."	1 Peter 1:19
Specially cared for	Exodus 12:6	"This is My beloved Son."	Matthew 3:17
Killed	Exodus 12:6	"Worthy is the Lamb that was slain."	Revelation 5:12
Eaten	Exodus 12:8	"Take, eat; this is My body."	Matthew 26:26
Sacrificed to spare others from judgment	Exodus 12:13	"For Christ our Passover also has been sacrificed."	1 Corinthians 5:7
Not one bone broken	Exodus 12:46	"Not a bone of Him shall be broken."	John 19:36

Jesus Christ, God's beloved Son, came to earth and lived a perfect life. The authorities crucified Him on the cross. His sacrifice paid for our sins. When we receive Him by faith as our personal Lord and Savior, He forgives us of our sins and makes us right with God. Truly the Passover Lamb provides a powerful picture of the future work of Christ.

By delivering the Hebrews from their slavery to the Egyptians, God will strategically position them during the Entering Era to more effectively proclaim this coming Messiah.

A LITTLE EXTRA

Often people attempt to disparage the Bible by seeking to challenge the validity of some of God's laws for today's society. For example they ask questions like: *If I eat shrimp on Saturday night, then should I not go to church on Sunday because shrimp makes a person unclean as in Leviticus 11:9–12? Would you get your neighbors to help stone your son to death if he rebelled against you today as God told the Israelites to do in Deuteronomy 21:18–21?*

By asking such questions, they demonstrate a common misunderstanding of the three different types of law in the Old Testament: moral law, ceremonial law, and civil law.

TYPE OF LAW	SCRIPTURE
Moral	Deuteronomy 5-11
Ceremonial	Deuteronomy 12-16
Civil	Deuteronomy 16-26

Two of these three categories, the ceremonial and civil law, no longer apply to us today. Christ fulfilled the ceremonial law when He died as the perfect sacrifice. See Hebrews 7:26–27 and 1 Peter 1:18–19. The civil law applied specifically to the nation of Israel, not to the governments of other peoples. The moral law of God communicated by the Ten Comandments, however, continues to this day because it is based upon the character of God.

THE TEN COMMANDMENTS

TOWARD GOD	SCRIPTURE	COMMANDMENT
"You shall love the Lord your God with all your heart, and with all your soul, and with all your mind." Mt. 22:37	Ex 20:3, Deu 5:7	1. You shall have no other gods before Me.
	Ex 20:4, Deu 5:8	2. You shall not make for yourself an idol.
	Ex 20:7, Deu 5:11	3. You shall not take the name of the Lord your God in vain.
	Ex 20:8, Deu 5:12	4. Remember the sabbath day to keep it holy.

TOWARD MAN	Ex 20:12, Deu 5:16	5. Honor your father and your mother.
"You shall love your neighbor as yourself."	Ex 20:13, Deu 5:17	6. You shall not murder.
	Ex 20:14, Deu 5:18	7. You shall not commit adultery.
Mt. 22:39	Ex 20:15, Deu 5:19	8. You shall not steal.
	Ex 20:16, Deu 5:20	9. You shall not bear false witness against your neighbor.
	Ex 20:17, Deu 5:21	10. You shall not covet.

FOR NEXT TIME

	OPTION 1 "An extremely busy week"	OPTION 2 "A little extra time"	OPTION 3 "Can't get enough"
DO	Next chapter – Era 4	Next chapter – Era 4	Next chapter – Era 4
READ		Average Readers: Read Joshua 1-6 about entering the Land	Average Readers: Read Joshua 1-6 about entering the Land
		Fast Readers: Add Judges 6-8 about Gideon	Fast Readers: Add Judges 6-8 about Gideon
		Speed Readers: Add Judges 13-16 about Samson	Speed Readers: Add Judges 13-16 about Samson
MEMORIZE (Choose one)			Third Era verse: Exodus 3:10
			Third application verse: Exodus 24:7
			Third Christ verse: Exodus 12:13
			Third personal verse: choose your own

JUST FOR LAUGHS

Little Joey's mom asked him what he learned in Sunday school. "Mom, our teacher told us how God sent Moses behind enemy lines on a rescue mission to lead the Israelites out of Egypt. When he got to the Red Sea he had his engineers build a pontoon bridge and all the people walked safely across it. Then he used his walkie-talkie to radio headquarters for reinforcements. They sent bombers to blow up the bridge and all the Israelites were saved." "Now Joey is that really what your teacher taught you?" his mother asked. "Well, no, but if I told it the way the teacher did, you would never believe it!"

* * *

The following unedited statements come from the writings of elementary school students. Pay particular attention to the spelling.

Moses led the Jews to the Red Sea where they made unleavened bread which is bread without any ingredients.

The Egyptians were all drowned in the dessert. Afterwards, Moses went up to Mount Cyanide to get the Ten Commandments.

Moses died before he ever reached Canada. Then Joshua led the Hebrews in the battle of Geritol.

* * *

A boy was sitting on a park bench with one hand resting on an open Bible. He was loudly exclaiming his praise to God. "Hallelujah! Hallelujah! God is great!" he yelled without worrying whether anyone heard him or not. Shortly after, along came a man who had recently completed some studies at a local university. Feeling himself very enlightened in the ways of truth and very eager to show this enlightenment, he asked the boy about the source of his joy. "Hey," asked the boy in return with a bright laugh. "Don't you have any idea what God is able to do? I just read that God opened up the waves of the Red Sea and led the whole nation of Israel right through the middle."

The enlightened man laughed lightly, sat down next to the boy and began to try to open his eyes to the "realities" of the miracles of the Bible. "That can all be very easily explained. Modern scholarship has shown that the Red Sea in that area was only ten inches deep at that time. It was no problem for the Israelites to wade across." The boy was stumped. His eyes wandered from the man back to the Bible laying open in his lap. The man, content that he had enlightened a poor, naïve young person to the finer points of scientific insight, turned to go. Scarcely had he taken two steps when the boy began to rejoice and praise louder than before. The man turned to ask the reason for the resumed jubilation. "Wow!" the boy exclaimed happily. "God is greater than I thought! Not only did He lead the whole nation of Israel through the Red Sea, He topped it off by drowning the whole Egyptian army in ten inches of water!"

ERA #4

ERA #4

ENTERING CANAAN

(JOSHUA–JUDGES)

You probably chose this book because you wanted to gain a better understanding of the Old Testament. Though few will retain all the details covered thus far, much less the details that follow, we all can remember the big picture if we just review often enough. So let's again take time to fill in Era #1's four key events, Era #2's four patriarchs, and from the last chapter Era #3's four titles. Don't forget to add the key word for each Old Testament historical era at the top of the chart.

ERA #1 THE HUMAN RACE OUT OF _____	ERA #2 THE HEBREW RACE INTO _____	ERA #3 _____ EGYPT

What does each book title from the third era mean?

Book title 1 – _____

Book title 2 – _____

Book title 3 – _____

Book title 4 – _____

Keep in mind that Old Testament history contains far more than the story of the Hebrews. Though vague initially, it reveals ever more clearly the coming Messiah, Jesus Christ. In the Nothing Era we learn the seed of woman will one day overcome the works of the serpent by crushing his head. From the Something Era we find that Christ will come from the seed of Abraham. God chose the Hebrew people not just to bless them, but for them to be a blessing by announcing to others the coming Christ. In the Exiting Era we discover that God uses the sacrificial lamb of their most famous feast, the Passover, to provide a powerful picture of what the Messiah would one day accomplish.

Recall three ways the Passover lamb of Exodus 12 pictures the coming Christ:

_____

_____

_____

In the Exiting Era God uses ten plagues to deliver the Hebrews from their Egyptian bondage. They escape through the parting of the Red Sea arriving at Mount Sinai. There they receive the Ten Commandments, the design for the Tabernacle, and instructions for the Levitical priests regarding five offerings and seven feasts. After counting their number they begin their march to enter the long-awaited Promised Land. Fear of the land's inhabitants, however, keeps them from entering so God requires them to wander in the wilderness for almost forty years until all of that disobedient generation dies. Having arrived at Moab east of the Jordan River, Moses counts the Hebrews for a second time as well as reminds them of the Ten Commandments for a second time. At the end of the Exiting Era, Moses has a new generation of Hebrews ready for a new era which we will call Entering Canaan.

Let's see what happens.

WHAT?

The fourth era covers the next three books of the Old Testament: Joshua, Judges, and Ruth. The latter describes a beautiful love story that occurs during this era between two of the forbearers of Christ. Only the books of Joshua and Judges add to the historical flow. Both of these focus on the theme of **conquering in Canaan.** Interestingly enough, they approach the subject from completely different perspectives.

Near the end of the Exiting Era, Moses clearly commanded the Hebrews to drive out all the peoples of the Promised Land and to destroy their places of worship. By completely eliminating the other people groups from the land (collectively known as Canaanites), the people of God would not only be protected physically, but also, and more importantly, spiritually.

Unfortunately, the people did not completely obey Moses' mandate and it cost them dearly. Let's see how.

HOW?

The book of Joshua details three successful military campaigns which give the Hebrews control of the land, but not total control. They allow some of the Canaanite people to remain along with their male and female gods; the Baals and the Asheroth. This incomplete action ultimately leads to terrible consequences. In the book of Judges we find latter generations of Hebrews turning away from the God of the Israelites in order to worship the gods of the Canaanites. (Check out Judges 2:11–13, 3:7, and 10:6.)

While the book of Joshua focuses on the Hebrews conquering the Canaanites physically, the book of Judges focuses on the Canaanites conquering the Hebrews spiritually. (You may need to go back and read that sentence again.) When God's people do turn from Him in order to worship the gods of Canaan, He allows the Hebrews to be taken captive. Please remember that God allows their captivity, not to pay them back, but to win them back. It works. When their misery becomes unbearable, the Hebrews cry out to the God who cares for them. Forever faithful, God raises up a leader (called a judge) to deliver them so they once again can walk in a love relationship with Him.

BOOK	FOCUS
Joshua	The Hebrews conquer the Canaanites physically.
Judges	The Canaanites conquer the Hebrews spiritually.

Understand, however, this doesn't happen just once. The cycle, presented generally in Judges 2:11–19, repeats itself in detail six times throughout the book of Judges! Each cycle follows the same **four steps**: the Hebrews do evil in the sight of God (sin), God allows them to be taken captive (suffering), they cry out to God (supplication), and God provides a judge to return them to a right relationship with Himself (salvation). They never seem to learn from their mistake and continue repeating the four-step cycle.

Let's put these four steps into chart-form to more easily see the six cycles found in the book of Judges.

THE BOOK OF JUDGES	STEP 1 SIN	STEP 2 SUFFERING	STEP 3 SUPPLICATION	STEP 4 SALVATION
CYCLE 1	"Israel did what was evil in the sight of the Lord" (3:7)	Under Mesopotamia (3:8)	"Israel cried to the Lord" (3:9)	"The Lord raised up a deliverer" (3:9) Othniel
CYCLE 2	"Israel again did evil in the sight of the Lord" (3:12)	Under the Moabites, Ammonites and Amalekites (3:13)	"Israel cried to the Lord" (3:15)	"The Lord raised up a deliverer" (3:15) Ehud

CYCLE 3	"Israel again did evil in the sight of the LORD" (4:1)	Under the Canaanites (4:2)	"Israel cried to the LORD" (4:3)	"The God of Israel has commanded" (4:6) Deborah and Barak
CYCLE 4	"Israel did what was evil in the sight of the LORD" (6:1)	Under the Midianites (6:1)	"Israel cried to the LORD" (6:7)	"The LORD is with you" (6:12) Gideon
CYCLE 5	"Israel again did evil in the sight of the LORD" (10:6)	Under the Philistines and the Ammonites (10:7)	"Israel cried out to the LORD" (10:10)	"The Spirit of the LORD came upon . . ." (11:29) Jephthah
CYCLE 6	"Israel again did evil in the sight of the LORD" (13:1)	Under the Philistines (13:1)	Not mentioned	"He shall begin to deliver Israel" (13:5,24) Samson

It's not as though God didn't warn them what would happen. Moses at the end of his life had told them (Numbers 33:50–52, 55–56) that if the Hebrews did not drive out all the Canaanite peoples then the Canaanites would become pricks in their eyes and thorns in their sides. Joshua at the end of his life also exhorted them to diligently seek to love the Lord. If they didn't, but rather served other gods, God promised to discipline them (Joshua 23:11, 16). In response the Hebrews (Joshua 24:16) had declared, "Far be it from us that we should forsake the LORD to serve other gods."

Yet even after promising to love the One who delivered them from Egypt and provided them with a land flowing with milk and honey, they left the Creator God in order to worship gods made by the hands of man.

What a warning to all of us! The serpent has not given up. What the deceiver began at the Garden of Eden, he continues to this day. We must stay alert and not succumb to his lies as the Hebrews did during the Entering Era.

WHERE?

The Entering Era begins in Moab located east of the Jordan River. There we find Joshua, after God appoints him as the new leader of the Hebrews, making preparations to enter the land of Canaan. When ready, Joshua and the people cross the river as God parts its waters the same way He parted the waters of the Red Sea. The twelve tribes of Israel have finally arrived in the Promised Land. Everything else that occurs in this era takes place in the land of **Canaan**.

Other Nations

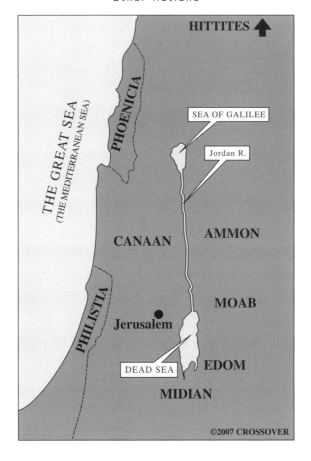

As the book of Joshua continues, it shows the Hebrews first conquering central Canaan. After dividing the land in half, they proceed with conquering southern Canaan and then northern Canaan. The twelve tribes then settle all over the Promised Land. Remember, however, pockets of resistance continue since the Hebrews do not totally drive out all the other people groups.

The Twelve Tribes of Israel

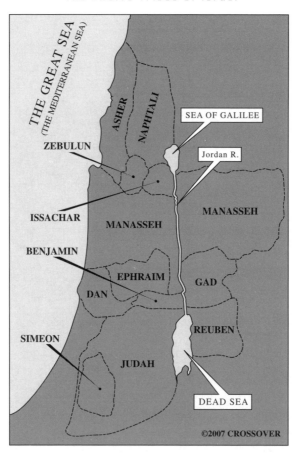

The six cycles in the book of Judges similarly cover all of Canaan. The judges Othniel and Ehud deliver the Hebrews in the southern part of Canaan,

Deborah and Barak in the northern part, Gideon in the center, Jephthah in the east, and Samson in the west.

WHEN?

If you remember, Moses died in 1405 BC bringing an end to the Exiting Era and a beginning to the Entering Era. Throughout this fourth era the people of God conquer and, after God allows them to be defeated because of worshipping the Canaanite gods, re-conquer various parts of the land. The cycle continues until this confederation of Hebrew tribes asks God to give them a king which He does in 1043 BC. The Entering Era thus lasts **from 1405 to 1043 BC.**

BOOK	NUMBER OF YEARS
Joshua	25 years
Judges	Almost 340 years

Since the book of Joshua covers only twenty-five years, one finds the vast majority of the Entering Era in the book of Judges. Conquering the land physically seems to have been much easier than conquering the land spiritually.

WHO?

Since the Entering Era covers several centuries we have many great men and women of God from whom we can learn more about growing spiritually. Six in particular stand out since the New Testament inducts them into the famous "Hall of Faith" found in chapter eleven of the book of Hebrews. From the book of Joshua we find two people who make the list: Joshua, the leader who took Moses' place, and Rahab, a prostitute. From the book of

Judges we discover that the Hall of Faith chapter also mentions the last four judges in the chart found on page 75 and 76 describing the four-step cycle.

Of the six we will focus on **Joshua**. Not only does he appear with Moses throughout the Exiting Era, but he leads the physical conquest of Canaan during this current era. So what can we learn from him?

Turn to chapter one of the book of Joshua and read the first two verses. The chapter (and era) begins with God transferring leadership of the Hebrew people to Joshua from Moses, who has recently died. For forty years Moses has led the people of Israel with miraculous results. He brought down the ten plagues of God upon Pharaoh, parted the Red Sea, requested manna from heaven to feed the people, received the Ten Commandments and the design for the tabernacle, and spoke to God face to face.

The Bible puts it like this when Moses died, "Since then no prophet has risen in Israel like Moses, whom the Lord knew face to face, for all the signs and wonders which the Lord sent him to perform in the land of Egypt against Pharaoh, all his servants, and all his land, and for all the mighty power and for all the great terror which Moses performed in the sight of all Israel" (Deuteronomy 34:10–12).

So how would you feel in Joshua's place if you had to follow Moses as the leader and conquer the Promised Land for which the Hebrews had been waiting almost seven hundred years? What kind of pressure would it put on you?

_____

_____

_____

Always one to care for the needs of His people, God provides Joshua with the assurance he needs in order to begin. In verses 3–5 God makes two promises to Joshua. One promise deals with Joshua having to fulfill Moses' role. The other promise concerns Joshua's responsibility to conquer Canaan. What does God promise him:

Regarding his role of following Moses?

_____

_____

Regarding his responsibility of conquering Canaan?

_____

_____

God did, however, communicate two prerequisites for Joshua in order for him to experience success. You find them in verses 6–9. The first requires Joshua to be strong and courageous. A very important prerequisite, God repeats it three times. What do you identify as the second prerequisite? Why do you think it is important?

_____

_____

_____

Let's give more attention to this second prerequisite. From what you know thus far about biblical history, to what part of the Old Testament does God refer when He cautions Joshua to do according to all that is written in the "book of the law"? Be specific.

_____

_____

God elaborates on the key to doing all that God has written in the book of the law. He explains that Joshua must first meditate on the Scriptures.

(We could call this a prerequisite for the prerequisite.) Find a dictionary and write down the definition for what it means to meditate.

_____

_____

To meditate on Scripture means to dwell on its meaning until you see how it personally applies to you. What a critical difference this makes in one's walk with God. Unfortunately, many Christians misunderstand spiritual maturity. They confuse learning Scripture with living Scripture. They think that since they know a lot about the Bible that they must, therefore, be very spiritual. For them the Christian life focuses on information for the head rather than on transformation of the heart.

The distinction between knowing and applying spiritual truth provides the catalyst for this practical section in each of the eras. We do not want to simply expand our knowledge of the Bible. While important, it falls short of what God desires from us. We cannot be satisfied until we grow in Christ-likeness. Putting it another way, we must make our ultimate objective not mastering the Word of God, but letting the Word of God master us.

What can you do to begin meditating on God's Word more intentionally?

_____

_____

It's a different way of thinking, isn't it? And Joshua realized it. Success in the eyes of God results from applying Scripture to our lives. Applying Scripture to our lives comes from meditating on its meaning in order to move it from our head to our hearts.

What lessons on Scripture can we learn from God's conversation with Joshua?

> *Lesson 1* – God's Word defines spiritual maturity in terms of the
> heart. It never limits spirituality to the realm of the head.

Lesson 2 – Moving Scripture from our head to our heart only comes with effort. Meditation starts the process moving in the right direction.

Lesson 3 – As we study our Bibles we must always consider (meditate on) what applications we can make, not just what information we can take.

Lesson 4 – Obeying Scripture from our hearts provides us with true success in life, that is, success from God's perspective.

Lesson 5 – A huge difference exists between us mastering the Word of God and letting the Word of God master us.

What other lessons can you add from this week's reading?

_____

_____

In the next era we will meet a man named David. In Psalms 1:2–3 he describes a godly man this way, "But his delight is in the law of the LORD, and in His law he meditates day and night. He will be like a tree firmly planted by streams of water, which yields its fruit in its season, and its leaf does not wither; and in whatever he does, he prospers."

Now let's add to our spiritual growth chart.

FOUR AREAS OF SPIRITUAL GROWTH	IMPROPER STEPS	PROPER STEPS
Fellowship with God	Era 1 – Hiding our sin from God or blaming it on others.	Era 5 –
Trust in God	Era 2 – Allowing fear to paralyze us.	Era 6 –
Obedience to God	Era 3 – Failing to follow-through on what God has commanded us to do.	Era 7 –

Hearing from God	Era 4 – Thinking that simply knowing Scripture is enough to be spiritually mature.	Era 8 –

WHY?

By the beginning of the Entering Era, word was starting to get out. The Hebrews served a different kind of god. What other god had completely humbled mighty Pharaoh through a series of ten plagues? Had anyone ever heard of a god powerful enough to part a sea and totally destroy a feared army in a matter of hours? Yet the Hebrews followed such a god, one named the Lord God.

For this reason, when Joshua sent two men as spies across the Jordan River to assess the strength of a city named Jericho, a Canaanite prostitute named Rahab (more about her in a moment) announced, "I know that the Lord has given you the land, and that the terror of you has fallen on us, and that all the inhabitants of the land have melted away before you. For we have heard how the Lord dried up the water of the Red Sea before you when you came out of Egypt. . . . When we heard it, our hearts melted and no courage remained in any man any longer because of you; for the Lord your God, He is God in heaven above and on earth beneath" (Joshua 2:9–11).

After possessing Canaan in the Entering Era, the Hebrews finally have a land from where they can proclaim to the nations God's desire to restore fellowship between the human race and Himself. If any doubt continues about God's love in the Old Testament for people groups other than the Hebrews, this era should erase it. The Entering Era contains two women, one a sinful Canaanite (Rahab) and the other a God-fearing Moabite (Ruth), who become part of the lineage of Christ. Check out Matthew 1:1–17 to see where they fit into the genealogy of Christ.

So the Entering Era gives the Hebrews a platform to announce the coming Deliverer to the nations. But does it add to our understanding about what this Messiah will do or be? Let's return to the story of Rahab.

It appears that the two spies Joshua sent to Jericho were not very good at espionage since the king hears of their presence in his city the same day they arrive. Not only does he know they entered his city, but he knows in whose house they went, that of Rahab. Yet Rahab, knowing the Hebrews serve the living God, hides the spies and deceives the king's men as to their location.

In return for her help the spies promise Rahab that if she will tie a scarlet thread in her window, all within her house would be spared when the Hebrew army takes the city. **This era pictures Christ as the scarlet thread,** just as the last era pictured Christ as the Passover Lamb. Because Rahab applies the thread to the window, God spares her from physical death. When the Hebrews applied the blood of the sacrificed lamb to their door, God spared them from physical death. When we apply Christ's blood to our heart, God spares us from spiritual death.

NOTE: The violence of the Old Testament, especially during this era, often confuses people. A superficial reading gives the impression that God does not love anyone but the Hebrews since He destroys so many different people groups through the army of Israel. Please understand that God did love these people and gave them ample opportunity to follow Him. The Canaanites knew about God because the parting of the Red Sea resulted in the news about Him to spread far and wide (Exodus 7:5 and 15:14–17). Rahab provides a perfect example of this fact since she proclaimed forty years after the Red Sea event, "For we have heard how the Lord dried up the water of the Red Sea before you when you came out of Egypt . . . for the Lord your God, He is God in heaven above and on earth beneath" (Joshua 2:10–11).

Had the Canaanites followed God, they would have experienced His blessings like Rahab and Ruth. They didn't, so He judged them and understandably so because of their wickedness (Deuteronomy 9:4). Deuteronomy 18:9–12 describes their practices, "When you enter the land which the Lord your God gives you, you shall not learn to imitate the detestable things of those nations. There shall not be found among you anyone who makes his son or his daughter pass through the fire [see Deuteronomy 12:31], one who uses divination, one who practices witchcraft, or one who interprets omens, or a sorcerer, or one who casts a spell, or a medium, or a spiritist, or one who calls up the dead. For *whoever* does these things is detestable to the LORD; and because of these detestable things the LORD your God will drive them out before you." Notice we italicized the preceding word emphasis. God does not limit His judgment to non-Hebrews. As we saw in the book of Judges He also judged the tribes of Israel whenever they turned from following Him. So God's judgment comes not from a lack of love on the part of God, but a lack of obedience on the part of man.

A LITTLE EXTRA

The book of Judges contains more judges than just those found in the six cycles. The chart below provides their names and the verses that tell about them.

THE TWELVE JUDGES OF ISRAEL (OR WAS IT THIRTEEN?) FOUND IN THE BOOK OF JUDGES

JUDGE	SCRIPTURE
Othniel	3:5-11
Ehud	3:12-30
Shamgar	3:31
Deborah and Barak	4:1-5:31
Gideon	6:1-8:32
Tola	10:1-2
Jair	10:3-5
Jephthah	10:6-12:7
Ibzan	12:8-10

Elon	12:11-12
Abdon	12:13-15
Samson	13:1-16:31

The boxes in the chart above total twelve. You will notice, however, that one of the boxes contains two names. Deborah and Barak served as judges together. When reading the book of Judges you will also come across one more name, Abimelech. We do not include him in the list of judges because he was a wicked oppressor of Israel rather than a righteous deliverer.

FOR NEXT TIME

	OPTION 1 "An extremely busy week"	OPTION 2 "A little extra time"	OPTION 3 "Can't get enough"
DO	Next chapter – Era 5	Next chapter – Era 5	Next chapter – Era 5
READ		Average Readers: Read 2 Samuel 1-11 about David Fast Readers: Add 1 Kings 1-11 about Solomon Speed Readers: Add 1 Samuel 1-15 about Samuel and Saul	Average Readers: Read 2 Samuel 1-11 about David Fast Readers: Add 1 Kings 1-11 about Solomon Speed Readers: Add 1 Samuel 1-15 about Samuel and Saul

MEMORIZE (Choose one)			Fourth Era verse: Joshua 1:2 Fourth application verse: Joshua 1:8 Fourth Christ verse: Joshua 2:21 Fourth personal verse: choose your own

JUST FOR LAUGHS

The Sunday school teacher asked the class to name the greatest miracle ever mentioned in the Bible. Little Johnny answered, "When Joshua told his son to stand still and he obeyed him" (See Joshua 10:12-13).

* * *

One elementary school student wrote the following:

Samson slayed the Philistines with the axe of the Apostles.

ERA #5

ERA #5

UNITED KINGS STAND

(1 SAMUEL–1 KINGS 11)

You have now made it half way through the eight eras. Hopefully, the puzzle of the Old Testament is beginning to take shape as we put together the picture's border within which all the other puzzle pieces fit.

As we review (again!) notice that each of the first four eras have four key items to recall. Era #1 contains four events, Era #2 four patriarchs, Era #3 four titles, and Era #4 four steps. Mastering these sixteen key items provides you with a fairly detailed chronological understanding of the plan God followed in order to bring the nations of the earth back into a right relationship with Himself. Consequently, given the opportunity, you now can explain this plan to others in a simple and clear way such that they, too, can appreciate what God accomplished in the Old Testament.

Well let's get to work. Fill in the sixteen items on the following chart, not forgetting to add the key word for each era at the top of the chart.

ERA #1 THE HUMAN RACE OUT OF _____	ERA #2 THE HEBREW RACE INTO _____	ERA #3 _____ EGYPT	ERA #4 _____ CANAAN

Using the above chart, write a brief history of the first four eras of the Old Testament.

_____

_____

_____

Now compare your summary of the first four eras to the summary Joshua writes in Joshua 24:1–13. He mentions the Nothing Era in verse 2, the Something Era in verses 3–5, the Exiting Era in verses 6–10, and the first half of the Entering Era in verses 11–13. Having read Joshua's version, what changes would you make to your initial summary?

_____

_____

Recall that the theme of the Bible demonstrates God receiving glory as He restores fellowship between the nations and Himself through His Son, Jesus Christ. As we work our way through each era, God slowly but surely reveals more and more about the main character of His book. We first learned that the Messiah would be born of a woman and would overcome the consequences of sin and the devil. We then realized that the Messiah would come through the Hebrew nation. In the last two eras we saw that the Passover Lamb and the scarlet cord provided God's people with a seminal understanding of what the Messiah would accomplish. His work would deliver from judgment those who sincerely trusted Him to deliver them.

Name the woman who placed the scarlet cord outside her window.

_____

In what city did she live? _____

Where can you find this story in the Old Testament? _____

When we last left the twelve tribes of Israel, they had conquered the Canaanites physically, but the Canaanites had conquered them spiritually. The people of God had not driven the Canaanites completely out of the Promised Land and as a result, the Hebrews turned away from the Creator God to worship the created gods, the Baals and Asheroth. Let's now proceed to the fifth era which we will call the United Era.

WHAT?

Turn for a moment to the section in the introductory chapter where we show how all the Old Testament Books connect to the historical books, or straight-edged pieces of the puzzle. On pages 10 and 11 you can see that the fifth era contains several books: 1 and 2 Samuel, part of 1 Kings, 1 Chronicles, part of 2 Chronicles, Psalms, Proverbs, Ecclesiastes, and Song of Solomon.

Notice, however, that only 1 Samuel, 2 Samuel, and the first half of 1 Kings add to the historical flow of the era. The book of 1 Chronicles and the first part of 2 Chronicles give commentary to the events of the previous three books. The other titles (Psalms, Proverbs, Ecclesiastes, and Song of Solomon) fall in the category of the Poetical Books. Two famous kings, who lived during this era and whom we will meet in a moment, wrote them.

So what happens in 1 Samuel, 2 Samuel, and the first half of 1 Kings that advances God's story? During this era the Hebrews complain that they do not have a king like the other nations. Indeed, God intentionally designed their government that way. He desired for the Hebrews to loyally follow Him as their King (1 Samuel 8:4–8) in order to draw the other nations into a relationship with Himself. Unfortunately, rather than wanting to influence the nations by following *the* King, the Hebrews wanted to imitate the nations by following *a* king. God begrudgingly gave them the king they wanted (1 Samuel 12:19–24), actually more than one.

Under the leadership of these kings, the people of God no longer form a loose confederation of twelve closely related tribes, but merge into a united kingdom. During this period of time, which we call the United Era, **the nation prospers** reaching the zenith of its power.

HOW?

During the United Era, God allows three different kings to rule His people: Saul, David, and Solomon. Let's take a closer look at what 1 Samuel, 2 Samuel, and 1 Kings say about these **three kings**.

KING	HISTORICAL CONTENT	HISTORICAL COMMENTARY
Saul	1 Samuel 8-15	1 Chronicles 10
David	1 Samuel 16-31	1 Chronicles 11-29
	2 Samuel 1-24	
	1 Kings 1-2	
Solomon	1 Kings 3-11	2 Chronicles 1-9

First Samuel begins by introducing Samuel, the last judge of Israel and the first in a long line of prophets. (He served as one of five oral prophets. These prophets did not write any of the books of the Old Testament as the literary prophets did.) Since Samuel serves as the judge or leader of Israel, he anoints Saul as the first king. Unfortunately, Saul has a heart problem. From the very beginning of his reign he places himself, rather than God, on the throne of his heart.

For example, before one battle he offered a sacrifice to God. Now offering a sacrifice did not create a problem, but how he offered it created one. Rather than waiting for a priest to offer the sacrifice, he offered it himself. Samuel later told him, "You have acted foolishly. You have not kept the commandment of the Lord your God . . . now your kingdom shall not endure. The Lord has sought out for Himself a man after His own heart."

Another time God told Saul to kill all the animals captured in a battle. Rather than kill everything, he keeps the best for himself. Not only that, but he builds a monument to himself rather than to God as the victor! When confronted by Samuel about his disobedience, he makes several interesting comments.

First, he lies by proclaiming he actually did obey what God wanted him to do. When asked about the bleating of the supposedly dead sheep, Saul blames others for not killing the animals. (Remind you of anyone?) Then he says he saved the animals to sacrifice to Samuel's God. Notice he did not say "his" God. Samuel responds to this excuse by explaining how much God values obedience more than sacrifice. Finally, when Samuel tells him that his action resulted in God rejecting him as king, Saul begs Samuel to go back with him and honor him before the people. If he had the right kind of heart, he would have focused more on what God thought of him than on what the people thought of him. Yet that captures his problem—he had more of a heart for himself than for God. In fact, the writer of 1 Chronicles (perhaps in disappointment with Saul) does not even mention King Saul when he provides color commentary about this era.

Halfway through 1 Samuel, this era introduces another character, David, one of the most famous people of the Bible. One thousand years later, the New Testament in Acts 13:22, 36 describes David as a man after God's own heart, one who did all of His will, and one who served the purpose of God in his generation. So how did he acquire such a sterling reputation?

David's story begins with Samuel anointing this shepherd boy to follow Saul as king. The very next chapter sheds light on his character. While Israel fights the Philistines, David brings some food to his brothers serving in the army. At the battle line he hears Goliath, a huge man, taunting the Israelites to a one-on-one, winner-take-all fight. So frightening an opponent, not one of the trained warriors dares to accept the intimidator's challenge. To everyone's surprise, David volunteers. Armed with nothing but a sling shot and five stones (some say five because Goliath had four brothers, see 2 Samuel 21:15–22), he slays the giant. What he tells Goliath before the fight communicates a lot. He says in 1 Samuel 17:45–46 that he fights "in the name of the Lord . . . that all the earth may know that there is a God in Israel."

Second Samuel continues the story. The first half of the book describes David's conquests. He becomes king, establishes Jerusalem as the capital of Israel, brings the Ark of the Covenant to this new capital city, and consolidates his kingdom through a series of military victories. (Do not confuse the Ark of the Covenant with Noah's ark. The latter was a boat that carried Noah and his family safely through the flood. The Ark of the Covenant was a box that contained the Ten Commandments, Aaron's rod that budded, and some manna, the food the Hebrews ate while wandering in the wilderness.)

Unfortunately, 2 Samuel does not continue on such a positive note. A turning point occurs in David's life (chapter 11) when he commits adultery and murder. The remainder of the book describes the consequences of his disobedience. His family goes through pain and agony from the rape of a daughter and the murder of a son. The kingdom experiences turmoil facing two revolts, famine, and a pestilence.

FOCUS	SCRIPTURE
David's Calling	1 Samuel 16-31
David's Conquests	2 Samuel 1-10
David's Compromise	2 Samuel 11
David's Consequences	2 Samuel 12-24
David's Conclusion	1 Kings 1-2

By the beginning of 1 Kings, David has reached the end of his life. As he lies dying, he makes it his priority to insure a smooth transition of the kingdom between him and the next king, his son Solomon.

Before turning to Solomon, we must return to the question above. How can Scripture describe an adulterer and murderer as a man after God's own heart? We will look at the answer more closely in the "Who" section below. For now we must let 1 Samuel 16:7 temporarily satisfy us. It says, "Do not look at his appearance or at the height of his stature . . . for God sees not as man sees, for man looks at the outward appearance, but the LORD looks at the heart." In the "Who" section we will see the contents of David's heart.

KING	DESCRIPTION
Saul	A heart devoted to himself
David	A heart devoted to God
Solomon	A heart devoted to God and himself

Chapters 2–11 of 1 Kings cover the time during the United Era that Solomon serves as king of Israel. Solomon begins ruling by diligently following the Lord. He builds a magnificent permanent temple, as opposed to

the portable tabernacle, in which to worship God. He even made room in the temple for the Gentiles (non-Hebrews) to come worship because he wanted the people from every nation to know God personally. In 1 Kings 8:43, 60 as Solomon dedicates the temple to God he prays, "Hear in heaven Your dwelling place, and do according to all for which the foreigner calls to You, in order that all the peoples of the earth may know Your name . . . so that all the peoples of the earth may know that the LORD is God."

Additionally, under Solomon's reign Israel reaches the zenith of her power. But the world does not remember Solomon for his power. People remember him for his wisdom, much of which you can find in the book of Proverbs.

DAVID'S POETRY	SOLOMON'S POETRY
	Proverbs
Psalms	Ecclesiastes
	Song of Solomon

Knowing the wisest course of action, however, does not necessarily mean pursuing the wisest course of action. Years before, Moses predicted the people would one day want a king so he set three specific limits on their ruler. In Deuteronomy 17:14–17 he forbade the kings to acquire great numbers of horses, take many wives, and accumulate large amounts of gold. Yet Solomon did all three (1 Kings 10:14–11:1) in excess.

Even though God warned him twice (1 Kings 11:9) about this, Solomon did not listen. As a result his foreign wives turned his heart away from God. He began to worship Ashtoreth, Milcom the detestable idol of the Ammonites which demanded the sacrifice of children, and Chemosh the god of the Moabites which also demanded children as burnt offerings. First Kings 11:6 provides a sad but fitting description of this king who started well but finished miserably. "Solomon did what was evil in the sight of the LORD, and did not follow the LORD fully, as David his father had done." Unlike his father, David, who whole-heartedly followed God, Solomon served God half-heartedly.

WHERE?

The events of the United Era all take place in the land of **Canaan**, now called the nation of Israel. By the end of Solomon's reign, the country looks like the map below.

Solomon's Israel

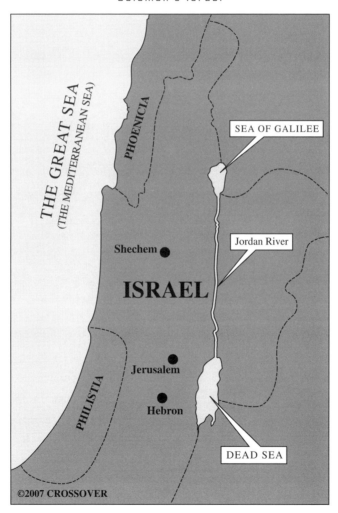

WHEN?

The advent of Saul's reign to the end of Solomon's reign clearly delineates the beginning and end of this fifth era of Old Testament history. It lasts from **1043 to 931BC** or between 112 to 114 years. This confuses some people since Saul reigned forty years (Acts 13:21), David forty years (1 Kings 2:11), and Solomon forty years (1 Kings 11:42) for a total of approximately one hundred and twenty years. (Approximately because the Scripture rounds off the number of years the kings ruled not choosing to be as precise as to the number of months and days.)

We can reconcile this apparent discrepancy when we remember that the reigns of David and Saul overlapped for about seven years (1 Kings 2:11).

WHO?

Though we find several very familiar names in the United Era, the amount of information devoted to **David** makes him an obvious choice to examine more closely. This era devotes the majority of its chapters (see the chart in the "How" section showing the historical content and commentary chapters) to his life.

But where do we start: his fight with Goliath, running for his life from jealous King Saul? We could learn from each of these stories and others. Yet as we saw in the "How" section, David's whole life pivots around one particular passage of the Bible. Before 2 Samuel 11 everything seems to come together for David. After 2 Samuel 11, however, all appears to fall apart. As mentioned earlier, in this chapter of Scripture David dishonors God in two hideous ways. He commits adultery with Bathsheba and murders her husband. Let's see what we can learn from David's disobedience that will encourage us to walk more closely with God. Since we already know *what* David does in these verses, let's begin by seeing what we can discover about *why* he does it.

Read Deuteronomy 17:14–17. We mentioned these verses earlier in reference to Solomon. What three restrictions did God place on a king of Israel?

_____

_____

Yet David violates one of the restrictions. Which of the prohibitions does David ignore? Read 2 Samuel 5:13.

_____

_____

Now read the next three verses, Deuteronomy 17:18–20, and answer these questions. What three actions was a king in Israel supposed to take when he occupied the throne of Israel? For what reasons did he take these actions?

_____

_____

_____

Whether David willfully disobeys what he knows God's Word says or he neglects over time to read God's Word and forgets what it says, we do not know. As a rule, however, a fall as violent as David's does not typically occur without a weakening process preceding it. In other words, when a house collapses, the wood has been rotting for quite a while. David struggled with lust. We know this not because he had many wives. Political circumstances possibly motivated these relationships. We can safely assume, however, the weakness of moral impurity in David's life because of all the concubines he added.

We do not mean to pick on David by identifying this flaw in his character. Every follower of Christ has a fatal flaw which if left unguarded threatens to destroy the person's life just as David's did. The key to protecting one's walk with God in this particular area can be found in Psalm 119:9–11 where the anonymous psalmist proclaims, "How can a young man keep his way pure? By keeping it according to Your word. With all my heart I have sought You; do not let me wander from Your commandments. Your word I have treasured in my heart, That I may not sin against You." Unfortunately, at some point along the way he dropped his guard leaving himself vulnerable to compromise.

David also set himself up for failure in another way. Not only did he leave his weakness unguarded (actually he encouraged the weakness), but also he found himself where he wasn't supposed to be. Read 2 Samuel 11:1. Where should King David be at this time of year and where do we find him?

_____

_____

As a result of his unguarded weakness and not being where he was supposed to be, when the temptation of Bathsheba presents itself, David chooses not to resist. Though he could have turned away when he saw the bathing woman, he chooses the same pattern Eve chose in Genesis 3. Read 2 Samuel 11:2–4 and complete the chart below with the corresponding verse.

PATTERN	EVE	DAVID
SAW SOMETHING FORBIDDEN	Gen 3:6	
DESIRED SOMETHING FORBIDDEN	Gen 3:6	
TOOK SOMETHING FORBIDDEN	Gen 3:6	

As we saw in our study on Moses, we can choose our sin, but we can't choose our consequences. Read 2 Samuel 11:5–27 and list some of the consequences of David's disobedience. Certainly you will notice the obvious ones like those found in verses 5 and 27, but look for the more subtle ones as well. For example, in verse 26 you discover that David's disobedience affects others, not just himself.

_____

_____

_____

At this point we need to again ask the question, why do the Scriptures call this adulterer and murderer a man after God's own heart? We find the answer in 2 Samuel 12. There God sends Nathan, a prophet, to rebuke David. Read verses 1–12. If you could only pick one of these 12 verses to summarize Nathan's rebuke of David, which verse would you choose and why?

_____

_____

_____

Remember 1 Samuel 16:7? David's response to Nathan reveals the key to David's heart. Read 2 Samuel 12:13. What does David say?

_____

_____

_____

Take a moment and compare David's response to the prophet Nathan's rebuke with Saul's responses to the prophet Samuel's rebukes and Solomon's response to God's rebuke. After reading the references found in the last column, fill in each king's response in the appropriate boxes.

KING	PROPHET'S REBUKE	KING'S RESPONSE (Scripture)
SAUL	1 Samuel 13:11	(1 Samuel 13:11-12)
SAUL	1 Samuel 15:17-19	(1 Samuel 15:20-21)
DAVID	2 Samuel 12:1-12	(2 Samuel 12:13)
SOLOMON	1 Kings 11:9	(1 Kings 11:10)

Notice that David's response drastically differs from the other kings. He realizes in the depth of his heart that his disobedient actions have grieved the Lord. He does not try to hide what he's done, nor does he try to blame someone else. He does not defend himself or make excuses. David takes full and complete responsibility for his ungodly actions.

Sometime after this sad episode David writes Psalm 51. Read it and answer the following questions noting the verse(s) of the psalm in parentheses beside your answers.

How does David describe God?

_____

_____

How does David describe his own actions and subsequent condition?

_____

_____

What various ways does David ask God to forgive him?

_____

_____

_____

When David asks God not to cast him away from His presence in Psalm 51:11, his request refers to his fellowship with God. Fellowship can best be described as that special love relationship we experience when nothing displeasing exists between us and God. When we do blow it and disobey God, our sin damages our fellowship with Him. Only confessing the disobedience brings restoration.

Now read one last passage, Psalm 32, another psalm written by David. How does David describe his restored fellowship with God?

_____

_____

_____

Let's apply what we've learned. Nothing exists in life more precious than your fellowship with God. So here's the question. Is there anything standing between you and God? If so, then find a private place and read Psalm 51 out loud to God. As you do, personalize it. Anytime you see words like sin, transgression, or iniquity, insert your own specific disobedience. When you finish, read Psalm 32 inserting personal pronouns like I, me, or my.

What lessons can we learn from David?

Lesson 1 – Our sinful tendencies will never go away in this life. We must vigilantly guard ourselves. We can expect nothing but disaster if we encourage or feed them.

Lesson 2 – When we do slip and disobey God, it damages our fellowship with Him.

Lesson 3 – Fellowship with God is our most precious possession on earth.

Lesson 4 – Only sincere confession of our sin restores our fellowship with God.

Lesson 5 – Once we confess our disobedience to God, regardless of how bad it seems, we can joyfully receive His forgiveness because the Messiah, Jesus Christ, paid for that sin at the cross.

What other lessons can you add from this week's reading?

_____

_____

_____

First Corinthians 1:9 says, "God is faithful, through whom you were called into fellowship with His Son, Jesus Christ our Lord." May we guard ourselves from anything that might disrupt our fellowship with God. If we do disobey, let's not hesitate a moment to honestly confess our disobedience so we might once again walk in close fellowship with Him.

For these final eras, when we add to our spiritual growth chart, we will focus on what we should do rather than what we should not do in order to grow in our walk with God.

FOUR AREAS OF SPIRITUAL GROWTH	IMPROPER STEPS	PROPER STEPS
Fellowship with God	Era 1 – Hiding our sin from God or blaming it on others.	Era 5 – Confessing our sin honestly and immediately to God.
Trust in God	Era 2 – Allowing fear to paralyze us.	Era 6 –
Obedience to God	Era 3 – Failing to follow-through on what God has commanded us to do.	Era 7 –
Hearing from God	Era 4 – Thinking that simply knowing Scripture is enough to be spiritually mature.	Era 8 –

WHY?

As we assemble the straight edges, we must never forget the overall picture of the Old Testament puzzle. In the Nothing Era we learned that God created man for fellowship with Himself. Adam's and Eve's disobedience, however, separated them from that glorious condition. From that point on, the theme of Scripture became God receiving glory by restoring fellowship between people from all nations and Himself through His Son, Jesus Christ.

From the very first era we saw God promised a Messiah to deliver not just the Hebrew race (they did not exist until the second era) but the human race from the consequences of its (our) disobedience. As each era progresses Scripture reveals more and more about this coming Messiah. Though a little vague until now, as we move into the fifth era things change. During this and the following three eras, we learn much about the coming sacrifice of the ultimate Passover Lamb. By the close of the Old Testament, Scripture reveals *how* Christ would die, *why* Christ would die, *when* Christ would die, and *where* Christ would die. Once you discover these passages, you will wonder why more people did not recognize Him when He finally arrived.

The United Era reveals **how Christ would die**. We learn this thrilling truth from another one of the psalms David wrote, Psalm 22. Please take a moment and read this psalm. As you do, you will clearly see God using David to communicate the future crucifixion of Christ. Realizing the Hebrews did not know about execution by crucifixion makes David's psalm all the more interesting. The chart below allows you to quickly see the specificity with which David reveals how Christ would die.

PSALM 22	CHRIST'S CRUCIFIXION
My God, my God, why hast Thou forsaken me? (v.1a)	My God, My God, why have You forsaken me? (Matthew 27:46b)
O my God, I cry by day, but You do not answer; And by night, but I have no rest. (v.2)	Now from the sixth hour darkness fell upon all the land until the ninth hour. (Matthew 27:45)
All who see me sneer at me. (v.7a)	And even the rulers were sneering at Him. (Luke 23:35b)
They separate with the lip, they wag the head, saying, "Commit yourself to the LORD; let Him deliver him; let Him rescue him, because He delights in him." (v.7b-8)	And those passing by were hurling abuse at Him, wagging their heads and saying, "You who are going to destroy the temple and rebuild it in three days, save Yourself! If You are the Son of God, come down from the cross." In the same way the chief priests also, along with the scribes and elders, were mocking Him, and saying, "He saved others; He cannot save Himself. He is the King of Israel; let Him now come down from the cross, and we shall believe in Him. He trusts in God; let God rescue Him now, if He delights in Him; for He said, 'I am the Son of God.'" The robbers who had been crucified with Him were also insulting Him with the same words. (Matthew 27:39-44)
For there is none to help. (v.11)	Then all the disciples left Him and fled. (Matthew 26:56b)
And all my bones are out of joint. (v.14)	Though not recorded in Scripture, studies demonstrate that when the executioners dropped the cross into the ground, that the victim's shoulders often popped out of joint.
And my tongue cleaves to my jaws. (v.15)	I am thirsty. (John 19:28b)

They pierced my hands and my feet. (v.16b)	And when they had crucified Him . . . (Matthew 27:35a)
They look, they stare at me. (v.17b)	And the people stood by, looking on. (Luke 23:35)
They divide my garments among them, and for my clothing they cast lots. (v.18)	They divided up His garments among themselves by casting lots. (Matthew 27:35)

Psalm 22 clearly predicts the crucifixion of the coming Christ.

Before we leave this psalm, let's look at one other truth it stresses. If you remember, Genesis 12:3 from the Something Era proclaims the Messiah would bless *all* the families of the earth. If you still doubt God's concern for people groups other than the Hebrews in the Old Testament, reread Psalm 22:27. It says, "*All* the ends of the earth will remember and turn to the LORD, And *all* the families of the nations will worship before You" (emphasis added). Throughout the whole Bible, not just the New Testament, God desires a love relationship with people from *every* people group.

A LITTLE EXTRA

During the Exiting Era while the people camped at Mount Sinai, God gave Moses instructions to construct the tabernacle. Scripture devotes eight chapters of the book of Exodus to what it should look like and another five chapters describing how they built it. This amount of Scripture seems reasonable since the tabernacle served as the focal point of the Hebrews' worship of God for hundreds of years. Since the people moved around a lot during the Exiting Era, the tabernacle was portable. The diagram on the following page shows the design of the tabernacle and give a general understanding of the arrangement of its contents. You may want to refer to Exodus 24:12–27:21 for the description and purpose of each item.

The Tabernacle

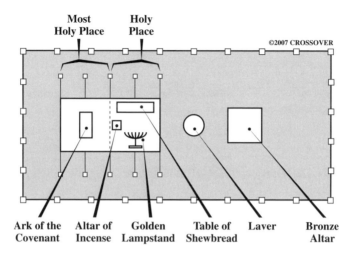

During our current era, the United Era, King David desired to establish a permanent place to worship God. Though he did not actually build what the Bible calls the temple, he provided everything for his son, Solomon, to build it. First Kings 5:1–8:66 give us an understanding of the magnificence of this structure. Unfortunately, invaders destroy it at the end of the next era. The diagram below shows the arrangement of the temple.

Solomon's Temple

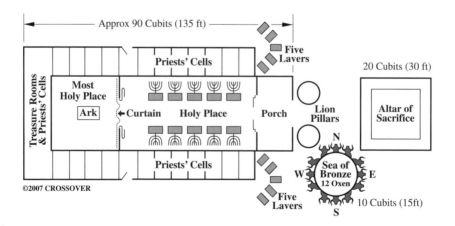

This chart may help in understanding the difference in the two places of Old Testament worship.

	TABERNACLE	TEMPLE
BUILDER	Moses	Solomon
FORMAT	Portable	Permanent
ERAS	Exiting and Entering Eras	United and Divided Eras

FOR NEXT TIME

	OPTION 1 "An extremely busy week"	OPTION 2 "A little extra time"	OPTION 3 "Can't get enough"
DO	Next chapter – Era 6	Next chapter – Era 6	Next chapter – Era 6
READ		Average Readers: Read 1 Kings 12-22 about how the nation is divided in two Fast Readers: Add 2 Kings 1-17 about what happens to the first half of the resulting two nations Speed Readers: Add 2 Kings 18-23 about what happens to the second half	Average Readers: Read 1 Kings 12-22 about how the nation is divided in two Fast Readers: Add 2 Kings 1-17 about what happens to the first half of the resulting two nations Speed Readers: Add 2 Kings 18-23 about what happens to the second half

MEMORIZE			Fifth Era verse:
(Choose one)			1 Samuel 8:6
			Fifth application verse: Psalm 51:2
			Fifth Christ verse: Psalm 22:16
			Fifth personal verse: choose your own

JUST FOR LAUGHS

The following unedited statements come from the writings of elementary school students. Pay particular attention to the spelling.

David was a Hebrew King who was skilled at playing the liar. He fought the Finkelsteins, a race of people who lived in biblical times.

Solomon, one of David's sons, had 300 wives and 700 porcupines.

ERA #6

ERA #6

DIVIDED KINGS FALL

(1 KINGS 12–2 KINGS 23)

As mentioned earlier, the first four eras have four key items to recall. Era #1 contains four events, Era #2 four patriarchs, Era #3 four titles, and Era #4 four steps. Eras #5–8 only require three key items to adequately summarize the historical events that occur during those times. For example, Era #5 contains the names of three kings. So as our custom, let's review the previous five Old Testament eras before beginning the sixth era. Fill in the five era names and the nineteen key items below.

ERA #1 THE HUMAN RACE OUT OF _____	ERA #2 THE HEBREW RACE INTO _____	ERA #3 _____ EGYPT	ERA #4 _____ CANAAN

```
┌─────────────────────┐
│       ERA #5         │
│     _____        │
│   KINGS STAND        │
├─────────────────────┤
│                      │
├─────────────────────┤
│                      │
├─────────────────────┤
│                      │
└─────────────────────┘
```

Keep in mind that we desire to know these events in order to better understand God's plan to bring the nations of the earth back into a right relationship with Himself through His Son, Jesus Christ.

What if someone challenged that the Old Testament revealed the coming Messiah? What would you say? Use the chart below as a guide to show how the first five eras reveal more and more clearly the coming of the Lord Jesus Christ.

ERA	1	2	3	4	5
REVEALS	Christ coming to _____	Christ coming from _____	Christ pictured as_____	Christ pictured as_____	_____ Christ would die
SCRIPTURE	Gen 3:15	Gen 12:2-3	Ex 12:13	Joshua 2:18	Psalm 22

The introduction of the above chart may have surprised you. Be forewarned, you will see it again. You don't want to get so focused on assembling the puzzle frame of the historical flow of the Old Testament that you forget the picture within it, Christ Himself.

With the story line of the first five eras fresh in our minds, we can now take a look at the next era.

WHAT?

Previously, during the United Era, the nation reaches the apex of its power. Unfortunately, when Solomon allowed his heart to turn away from God to follow the gods of the surrounding nations, his choice resulted in negative consequences. (Never forget: you can choose your sin, but not your consequences.) God judged Solomon's disobedience by proclaiming He would **separate the nation** into two kingdoms after Solomon's death. That's exactly what happened. Consequently, we call this era the Divided Era.

Now in this era things can get a little complicated very quickly. Two reasons make this so. First, the Divided Era contains more books of the Bible than any other era: part of 1 Kings, 2 Kings, and 2 Chronicles, and all of Isaiah, Jeremiah, Lamentations, Hosea, Joel, Amos, Obadiah, Jonah, Micah, Nahum, Habakkuk, and Zephaniah. If you refer to the chart on page 12 you will notice that only the information found in 1 Kings and 2 Kings adds to the historical framework of our puzzle. You will also notice that this era contains most of the Prophetical books of the Old Testament.

A second reason exists that can make the Divided Era seem a bit overwhelming at times. It deals not with three Hebrew kings like the last era, but with thirty-nine Hebrew kings. Add to this list the names of the literary prophets mentioned above plus a couple of oral prophets like Elijah and Elisha and the number of personalities becomes quite intimidating. The sheer number of uncommon names (like Jehoshaphat) can confuse even the sharpest of minds.

But don't worry. We will organize the people and events of the Divided Era in such a way as to make sense of it all.

HOW?

As mentioned above, eras 5 to 8 have three key items that help us remember what occurred during those particular time periods. The United Era contained three kings: Saul, David, and Solomon. This era, the Divided

Era contains **three kingdoms**, Israel, Judah, and Assyria. Let's see what role these three kingdoms play.

The previous era ended with chapter 11 of 1 Kings. In that chapter Solomon's non-Hebrew wives influenced him to follow their gods such that he no longer whole-heartedly devoted himself to worshipping the living God. Though God warned him, he did not listen. As a consequence, God told Solomon that his disobedience would divide the kingdom after his death. In 1 Kings 12, the first chapter of this current era, the kingdom splits.

Here's how it happened. Upon Solomon's death the twelve tribes assembled to crown Solomon's son, Rehoboam, as their king. While together the people asked Rehoboam to make life easier for them than Solomon had. (Solomon had required the people to pay high taxes and perform hard labor in the construction of his palace and the temple.) Rather than heed the wise advice of his father's counselors, Rehoboam listened to the suggestions of his young friends and declared he would make life more difficult for his people.

Obviously, this did not go over very well. The ten tribes in the north of Israel revolted and crowned a new king for themselves, Jeroboam. The remaining two tribes, Judah and Benjamin, located in the south kept Rehoboam as their king. So now we have two of the three kingdoms that define this era: *Judah* and *Israel*.

KINGDOM	Israel	Judah
KNOWN ALSO AS	Northern Kingdom	Southern Kingdom
TRIBES	10	2
CAPITAL CITY	Samaria	Jerusalem
FIRST KING	Jeroboam	Rehoboam

But what about the third kingdom; from where does it come? First a little background. After Jeroboam became king he realized he had one major problem if he wanted to keep his kingdom for the long-term. He knew he needed to offer a substitute for the religious activity that occurred in Jerusalem, the capital of Judah. He rightly feared that if his people regularly returned to that city to offer sacrifices that they ultimately might realign themselves with Rehoboam. If that happened, not only would he be out of a job, but he would probably be running for his life.

He solved his problem by creating two golden calves. (Remind you of anyone?) He then told the people that the two calves had delivered them from Egypt and to worship them through feasts and sacrifices rather than going all the way to Jerusalem to worship the God of Judah. To make worship of the golden calves accessible, he placed one at Dan in the north of Israel and one at Bethel in the south.

In spite of warnings from prophets like Amos and Hosea, the people of Israel continued worshipping these idols for the next two centuries. Second Kings 17:5–23 describes what happens next and why. In this passage the third kingdom appears. God sends Assyria, one of the most powerful military forces of the world of that time, as judgment for Israel's disobedience. The Assyrian army carries off the people of Israel and disperses them throughout their empire (2 Kings 17:6). By marrying the people who live in these territories the ten northern tribes basically disappear and become known as the lost ten tribes of Israel.

Judah, however, continues to exist after the fall of Israel for more than a century. We learn what happens to the two tribes of this southern kingdom in the next era.

THREE KINGDOMS	HISTORICAL CONTENT	HISTORICAL COMMENTARY
Judah and Israel	1 Kings 12 – 2 Kings 16	2 Chronicles 10-28
Assyria captures Israel	2 Kings 17	
Judah only	2 Kings 18-23	2 Chronicles 29-35

Before moving to the next section, perhaps we should clear up something. People sometimes get a little confused when the Bible speaks of "Israel." During the United Era the Hebrews called their country Israel. After the country divides, the northern ten tribes continue to call their new country Israel. The southern two tribes, however, call their new country Judah after the bigger of the two tribes. To complicate matters, after Assyria conquers the northern kingdom, Judah takes the name Israel. So depending on the era, Israel can mean twelve tribes, ten tribes, or two tribes.

Israel	Israel	Israel, formerly Judah
(12 tribes)	(10 tribes)	(2 tribes)
Before the Divided Era	During the Divided Era	After the Divided Era

Notice the chart above. Remembering within which era a Bible passage falls clears up the potential confusion.

WHERE?

The vast majority of the events of the Divided Era occur in the land of **Canaan**. The next map shows the two separate kingdoms of Israel and Judah.

Divided Kingdom

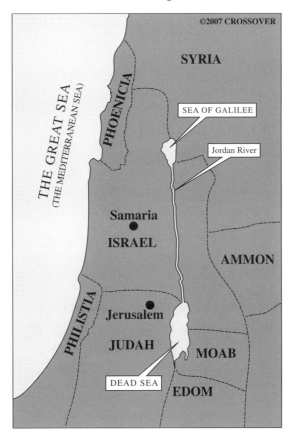

The map on the following page presents the third kingdom of this era, that of Assyria. Remember, however, that they never conquer Judah.

WHEN?

The Divided Era begins with the death of Solomon, the last of the three kings who ruled over all twelve tribes during the United Era. We set that date, as we learned in the previous era, at 931 BC. Before we determine the year that the Divided Era ends, we must note one other very important date: the

The Assyrian Empire
900-607 BC

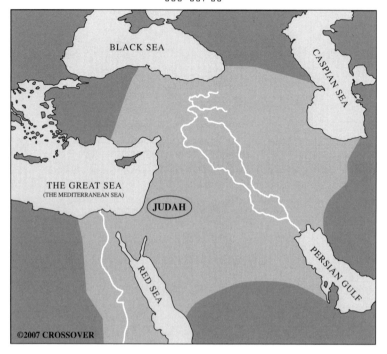

year Israel, as in the northern ten tribes, ceased to exist. Assyria conquered Israel and dispersed the Israelites throughout their realm in 722 BC.

	ISRAEL (10 Tribes)	JUDAH (2 Tribes)
ENDING DATE OF KINGDOM	722 BC	586 BC
DURATION OF KINGDOM	209 years	345 years
CONQUERER OF KINGDOM	Assyria	Find out next era!
DOWNFALL OF KINGDOM	Worshipping the golden calves	Find out next era!

Judah, the southern kingdom, continues for many more years. Not until 586 BC does Judah come to an end. (We won't reveal how it ends until the next era, though you can probably make a good guess as to why it ends. If you need a couple of hints: Why did God divide the United Kingdom in two? Why did God send Assyria to conquer the northern kingdom? If you know the answers to these two questions, then you can accurately guess why Judah falls.) So the overall time frame for the Divided Era lasts from **931 to 586 BC.**

WHO?

With so many personalities from whom to choose during the Divided Era, where do we start? **Hezekiah** seems a great choice for several reasons. First, out of the thirty-nine total kings between the northern and southern kingdoms, only a few walked with God. Hezekiah stands out as one of them. Next, he reigned in Judah during the tumultuous time when Assyria conquered Israel and threatened Hezekiah's southern kingdom as well. By studying Hezekiah in this section, we can more easily remember the approximate time of the northern kingdom's fall and dispersion. Finally, of the many prophets who confronted and comforted God's people during this era, one of the most famous, the prophet Isaiah, labored beside Hezekiah.

So what can we learn from him that will encourage our own walks with God? Though a fairly long passage about Hezekiah, 2 Kings 18–19 teaches us the proper steps to take to express true trust in God. Let's see what we can discover.

Chapter 18 begins with a brief biography on King Hezekiah. Read the first eight verses and note what you learn about the following.

Hezekiah's reign (verses 1–2): _____

_____

Hezekiah's righteous actions (verses 3–4): _____

_____

Hezekiah's walk with God (verses 5–8): _____

_____

Take a closer look at verse 5. It provides another good reason for wanting to study Hezekiah. How many kings of Judah trusted God more than him?

_____

_____

Understanding the godly character of this righteous king of Judah readies us to look at the events that take place in the rest of this passage. The rest of chapter 18 provides the context for what we learn about Hezekiah in chapter 19.

As we continue our search in chapter 18 we find that it mentions all three kingdoms of the Divided Era: Israel, Judah, and Assyria. Read verses 9–12. (Note that Samaria here refers to a city, the capital city of Israel the northern kingdom. It is not the province of Samaria that you read about in the New Testament during the time of Jesus.) What takes place in these verses and why?

_____

_____

_____

In verses 13–16 the same empire that invaded and conquered Israel now invades Judah and captures its fortified cities. Hezekiah agrees to pay tribute in order to appease the aggressor. What does it cost him and where does he get the silver and gold he has to pay?

_____

_____

The silver and gold King Hezekiah pays Sennacherib, the king of Assyria, satisfies him but only temporarily. Verses 17–18 tell us that he soon invades Judah again. Before attacking Jerusalem, however, he sends three of his diplomats (along with a huge army for motivational purposes) to work out a deal with their three Judean counterparts.

In verses 19–25 the Assyrian spokesman, Rabshakeh (probably a title, not a person's name), tries to persuade Judah to surrender without a fight by making two arguments: the first from a military perspective and the second from a spiritual point of view. Rabshakeh declares that relying on a military alliance with Egypt will not bring victory, nor will depending on the aid of the Lord God. Rabshakeh even goes as far as to say that Hezekiah's God gave the Assyrians the approval to destroy Judah in the first place. Talk about psychological warfare! Since the Assyrians had recently destroyed Israel, this definitely gets the attention of the three Judean diplomats.

The good guys in verse 26 beg Rabshakeh not to continue the negotiations in the Judean language since his threats bring fear to the people who are standing upon the defensive wall encircling the city and listening to every word he utters. They ask if they can negotiate in a different tongue so their countrymen cannot understand.

Rabshakeh realizes in verses 27–37 he must be really getting to them, so instead of switching to another language, he starts shouting so even more of the people can hear what he has to say. He announces that if Jerusalem refuses to surrender that the siege will doom them to eating their own dung and drinking their own urine. (Now that will make one pause and reevaluate his position.) Yet, if they do submit to the king of Assyria, then they would live a peaceful life but in another country. (The Assyrians liked to move their captured peoples to different places in order to quell rebellions. See 2 Kings 17:24 and Ezra 4:2, 10.)

Rabshakeh, a skilled negotiator, focuses on the one concession he needs the people of Judah to make. If they give in on this one point, he will secure his mission of taking Jerusalem without a struggle. Read verses 29–30. What compromise does Rabshakeh want them to make?

_____

_____

By the end of the chapter the Judean diplomats in great anxiety return to Hezekiah and report the situation. Now, you may be wondering why we looked at chapter 18 in so much detail. We did so because it helps us see why Hezekiah's response to his representatives is so amazing. In 2 Kings 19:1–7 Hezekiah takes three initial steps. He humbles himself before the Lord by tearing his clothes and covering himself with sackcloth. Next he goes into the house of the Lord. Finally, he sends a message to his friend, the prophet Isaiah, asking him to pray.

Meanwhile, Rabshakeh returns in verses 8–13 with a message from the king of Assyria. Look at verse 10. What is the heart of the Assyrian king's letter?

_____

_____

In verses 14–19, after reading the message Hezekiah returns to the house of the Lord (the temple) and prays a powerful prayer. Read verse 15. How does he describe God?

_____

_____

As Hezekiah prays to God (verse 16), who does he say the king of Assyria is attacking?

_____

What reason in verses 17–18 does Hezekiah give God to explain why the Assyrians were able to defeat so many nations and cast their gods into the fire?

_____

_____

Read verse 19. Why did Hezekiah ask God to deliver his city from the Assyrians?

_____

_____

SCRIPTURE	HEZEKIAH'S FAITH
2 Kings 18:5	"He trusted in the LORD"
2 Kings 18:22	"We trust in the LORD"
2 Kings 18:30	"Nor let Hezekiah make you trust in the LORD"
2 Kings 18:32	"The LORD will deliver us"
2 Kings 19:1	"He entered the house of the LORD"
2 Kings 19:4	"Therefore, offer a prayer"
2 Kings 19:10	"Your God in whom you trust"
2 Kings 19:14	"He went up to the house of the LORD"

2 Kings 19:15	"Hezekiah prayed before the LORD"
2 Kings 19:19	"O LORD our God, I pray, deliver us"
2 Kings 19:20	"Because you have prayed to Me"

In verses 20 and 34 the prophet Isaiah tells Hezekiah that because he prayed the city would be safe. God would rout the Assyrians for His own name's sake. Read verses 35–37. Describe the victory the Lord provided.

_____

_____

_____

Though we had to work through a lot of verses, we gained some very valuable insights to help us grow in our walks with Christ. Let's look at some of the lessons we can learn from King Hezekiah.

Lesson 1 – The God of the Bible is real and wants us to depend on Him to meet all our needs.

Lesson 2 – Our first response to bad news needs to be one of prayer.

Lesson 3 – Regardless of how big the problem seems, God is bigger.

Lesson 4 – Fear can paralyze humans, but the prayer of faith can mobilize God.

Lesson 5 – If we want to know how much we truly trust in God, as opposed to our own abilities and resources, all we need to do is to examine our prayer life.

What other lessons can you add from this week's reading?

_____

_____

Are you worried about something right now because you are not trusting in God to take care of you? Philippians 4:6–7 says, "Be anxious for nothing, but in everything by prayer and supplication with thanksgiving let your requests be made known to God. And the peace of God, which surpasses all comprehension, will guard your hearts and your minds in Christ Jesus." May we seek to be men and women of prayer, trusting God to meet all of our needs.

We can now add to our spiritual growth chart another proper step we can take to move forward in our walk with Christ.

FOUR AREAS OF SPIRITUAL GROWTH	IMPROPER STEPS	PROPER STEPS
Fellowship with God	Era 1 – Hiding our sin from God or blaming it on others.	Era 5 – Confessing our sin honestly and immediately to God.
Trust in God	Era 2 – Allowing fear to paralyze us.	Era 6 – Making prayer our first choice, not our last chance.
Obedience to God	Era 3 – Failing to follow-through on what God has commanded us to do.	Era 7 –
Hearing from God	Era 4 – Thinking that simply knowing Scripture is enough to be spiritually mature.	Era 8 –

WHY?

While the Nothing Era only vaguely revealed that the Messiah would one day come to crush the head of the serpent, the United Era made several very specific revelations. Psalm 22:16 clearly stated that a band of evildoers would one day pierce His hands and feet. So in the last era we learned how the coming Christ would die.

Isaiah, the prophet who so faithfully served King Hezekiah, wrote the book of Isaiah. Chapter 53 of that book presents the most vivid portrait of Christ found anywhere in the Old Testament. Much like Psalm 22, it predicts the coming events surrounding the crucifixion, even adding to them. Consider some of the prophecies in the chart on the next page remembering that Isaiah wrote them over seven hundred years before the Lord Jesus Christ came to earth.

Yet, Isaiah's passage goes further than just revealing HOW Christ would die. He clearly reveals in verses 4-6 WHY Christ would die. By circling all the first person pronouns (we, our, and us) in these three verses and putting them together, you will make an interesting discovery.

He Himself bore	our griefs
He carried	our sorrows
He was pierced through for	our transgressions
He was crushed for	our iniquities
The chastening fell on Him for	our well-being
By His scourging	we are healed
	All of us like sheep have gone astray, each of us has turned to his own way . . .
But the Lord has caused to fall on Him	the iniquity of us all

Do you notice a pattern in the above chart? Isaiah 53:4–6 answers **why Christ would die**. He came to die for all of us, each and every one, so that we might once again be back in a right relationship with God. First Peter 3:18 puts it this way, "For Christ also died for sins . . . the just for the unjust, so that He might bring us to God."

ISAIAH 53	CHRIST'S CRUCIFIXION
He has no stately form or majesty that we should look upon Him, nor appearance that we should be attracted to Him. (v.2)	They spat on Him, and took the reed and began to beat Him on the head. (Matthew 27:30)
He was despised and forsaken of men. (v.3)	Then all the disciples left Him and fled. (Matthew 26:56)
But He was pierced through for our transgressions. (v.5)	And when they had crucified Him . . . (Matthew 27:35)
And by His scourging we are healed. (v.5)	But after having Jesus scourged . . . (Matthew 27:26)
He was oppressed and He was afflicted, yet He did not open His mouth. (v.7)	The high priest stood up and said to Him, "Do You not answer? What is it that these men are testifying against You?" But Jesus kept silent. (Matthew 26:62-63)
Like a lamb that is led to slaughter. (v.7)	Behold, the Lamb of God who takes away the sin of the world. (John 1:29)
He was cut off out of the land of the living, for the transgression of my people, to whom the stroke was due (v.8)	For Christ also died for sins . . . the just for the unjust, so that that He might bring us to God. (1 Peter 3:18)
His grave was assigned with wicked men, yet He was with a rich man in His death. (v.9)	. . . there came a rich man from Arimathea . . . and Joseph took the body . . . and laid it in his own new tomb. (Matthew 27:57-60)
He had done no violence, nor was there any deceit in His mouth. (v.9)	. . . the whole Council kept trying to obtain false testimony against Jesus, so that that they might put Him to death. They did not find any, even though many false witnesses came forward. (Matthew 26:59-60)
My Servant, will justify the many, as He will bear their iniquities. (v.11)	. . . having now been justified by His blood, we shall be saved from the wrath of God through Him. (Romans 5:9)
And was numbered with the transgressors. (v.12)	They crucified two robbers with him. (Mark 15:27)
Yet He Himself bore the sin of many. (v.12)	And He Himself bore our sins in His body on the cross. (1 Peter 2:24)

When we put together the puzzle of the Old Testament, we see God receiving glory by restoring fellowship between all people groups and Himself through His Son, Jesus Christ. Though the vast majority of the people in the Divided Era ignored this great theme of Scripture, many people during this era continued taking the blessing of God to the nations. The great prophets Elijah and Elisha showed God's love for the non-Hebrews, the widow of Zarephath and Naaman, by reaching out to them. Most people associate Jonah with the whale, but fail to realize he went to announce God's love to the Assyrians, a people known for their incredible cruelty which included pulling captives' tongues out by the roots, skinning people alive and stretching the skins on the city walls, burning children alive, impaling victims through the chest and hoisting them up on top of long poles, and amputating feet, hands, noses, and ears. From the beginning of the Old Testament to the end of the New Testament, God demonstrates His unfailing love for us, all of us.

A LITTLE EXTRA

Since so many kings and prophets fill the years of the Divided Era, the following two charts will help organize them for you. Listed in chronological order, the charts identify the character of the king, where he occurs in Scripture, and the prophet or prophets that served during the same time period. Notice that all nineteen of the kings of Israel ruled with a wicked heart. Eight, however, of Judah's twenty kings did right in the sight of the Lord. Notice, too, in addition to the literary prophets, we note two famous oral prophets, Elijah and Elisha, since they dominate much of this era.

TWO SETS OF KINGS AND PROPHETS

KINGS OF **ISRAEL**	HEART	SCRIPTURE	PROPHET
1. Jeroboam	Evil	1 Kings 12:20-14:20	
2. Nadab	Evil	1 Kings 15:25-31	

3. Baasha	Evil	1 Kings 15:32-16:7	
4. Elah	Evil	1 Kings 16:8-14	
5. Zimri	Evil	1 Kings 16:15-20	
6. Omri	Evil	1 Kings 16:21-28	
7. Ahab	Evil	1 Kings 16:28-22:40	Elijah (oral)
8. Ahaziah	Evil	1 Kgs 22:51-2 Kgs 1:18	Elijah (oral)
9. Jehoram (Joram)	Evil	2 Kings 3:1-9:26	Elisha (oral)
10. Jehu	Evil	2 Kings 9:1-10:36	Elisha (oral)
11. Jehoahaz	Evil	2 Kings 13:1-9	Elisha (oral)
12. Jehoash	Evil	2 Kings 13:10-14:16	Elisha (oral)
13. Jeroboam II	Evil	2 Kings 14:23-29	Jonah, Amos, Hosea
14. Zechariah	Evil	2 Kings 15:8-15:12	Hosea
15. Shallum	Evil	2 Kings 15:13-15	Hosea
16. Menahem	Evil	2 Kings 15:16-22	Hosea
17. Pekahiah	Evil	2 Kings 15:23-26	Hosea
18. Pekah	Evil	2 Kings 15:27-31	Hosea
19. Hoshea	Evil	2 Kings 17:1-6	Hosea

KINGS OF **JUDAH**	HEART	SCRIPTURE	PROPHET
1. Rehoboam	Evil	1 Kings 12:1-14:31	
2. Abijam	Evil	1 Kings 15:1-8	
3. Asa	Good	1 Kings 15:9-24	
4. Jehoshaphat	Good	1 Kings 22:41-50	
5. Jehoram	Evil	2 Kings 8:16-24	Obadiah
6. Ahaziah	Evil	2 Kings 8:25-9:28	
7. Athaliah (woman)	Evil	2 Kings 11:1-20	
8. Joash (Jehoash)	Good	2 Kings 12:1-21	Joel
9. Amaziah	Good	2 Kings 14:1-20	
10. Azariah (Uzziah)	Good	2 Kings 15:1-7	Isaiah
11. Jotham	Good	2 Kings 15:32-38	Isaiah, Micah
12. Ahaz	Evil	2 Kings 16:1-20	Isaiah, Micah
13. Hezekiah	Good	2 Kings 18:1-20:21	Isaiah, Micah
14. Manasseh	Evil	2 Kings 21:1-18	Nahum
15. Amon	Evil	2 Kings 21:19-26	

16. Josiah	Good	2 Kings 22:1-23:30	Zephaniah, Jeremiah
17. Johoahaz	Evil	2 Kings 23:31-34	Jeremiah
18. Jehoiakim	Evil	2 Kings 23:35-24:7	Jeremiah, Habakkuk
19. Johoiachin (Jeconiah)	Evil	2 Kings 24:8-16	Jeremiah
20. Zedekiah	Evil	2 Kings 24:17-25:30	Jeremiah

FOR NEXT TIME

	OPTION 1 "An extremely busy week"	OPTION 2 "A little extra time"	OPTION 3 "Can't get enough"
DO	Next chapter – Era 7	Next chapter – Era 7	Next chapter – Era 7
READ		Average Readers: Read 2 Kings 24-25 about what happens to Judah Fast Readers: Add the book of Daniel about the prophet Daniel Speed Readers: Add Ezekiel about the prophet Ezekiel	Average Readers: Read 2 Kings 24-25 about what happens to Judah Fast Readers: Add the book of Daniel about the prophet Daniel Speed Readers: Add Ezekiel about the prophet Ezekiel
MEMORIZE (Choose one)			Sixth Era verse: 2 Kings 24:14 Sixth application verse: 2 Kings 18:5 Sixth Christ verse: Isaiah 53:5 Sixth personal verse: choose your own

JUST FOR LAUGHS

A Sunday school teacher said to her class, "We have been learning how powerful kings and queens were in the Bible. But, there is a higher power. Can anybody tell me what it is?" One child blurted out, "Aces!"

* * *

The Sunday school teacher was carefully explaining the story of Elijah the Prophet and the false prophets of Baal. She explained how Elijah built the altar, put wood upon it, cut the cow in pieces, and laid it upon the altar. Then, Elijah commanded the people of God to fill four barrels of water and pour it over the altar. He had them do this four times. "Now," said the teacher. "Can anyone in the class tell me why the Lord would have Elijah pour water over the cow on the altar?" A little girl in the back of the room started waving her hand, "I know, I know," she said. "To make the gravy!"

ERA #7

ERA #7

SCATTERED JUDAH

(2 KINGS 24–2 KINGS 25)

By faithfully reviewing, you now grasp the key items (events, patriarchs, meanings of book titles, steps in the cycle, kings, and kingdoms) in each of the first six eras. You also can confidently recall the names of those eras. Diligently working on these last two lessons will complete your understanding of what God accomplished during the Old Testament. Fortunately, the last four eras only require three key items each in order to identify the key items of those times, for example, the three kingdoms of the Divided Era. So without getting any help, once again fill in the items associated with the first six eras.

ERA #1	ERA #2	ERA #3	ERA #4
THE HUMAN RACE OUT OF _____	THE HEBREW RACE INTO _____	_____ EGYPT	_____ CANAAN

ERA #5	ERA #6
_____ KINGS STAND	_____ KINGS FALL

Although the above chart summarizes what God did during these eras, we must never forget why God did it: to restore fellowship between the nations and Himself. Because man's disobedience separated him from his Lord, God had to deal with man's sin in order to reconcile the broken relationship. But how did He do this? He did so through His Son, Jesus Christ. Sacrificing the ultimate Passover Lamb had always been God's plan to provide the nations with the blessing of His forgiveness. Though nebulous during the earlier eras, the Old Testament progressively reveals with greater clarity the coming Messiah. To help plant this truth deeply in your heart and mind, fill in the following chart.

ERA	REVEALS	SCRIPTURE
1	Christ coming to _____	Gen 3:15
2	Christ coming from _____	Gen 12:2,3
3	Christ pictured as _____	Ex 12:13
4	Christ pictured as _____	Josh 2:18
5	_____ Christ would die	Ps 22
6	_____ Christ would die	Isa 53:4-6

Hopefully at this point you see how the pieces of the puzzle frame all fit together and you have greater clarity on the content of the Old Testament. Though the seventh era does not contain a great amount of information within the historical books of the Bible, it does contain a very significant event. Let's see what happens during the Scattered Era.

WHAT?

In the last lesson we took an in-depth look at the life of Hezekiah, perhaps the greatest king during the Divided Era. Unfortunately, the son who took his place, Manasseh, did not walk in his steps but rather chose to do evil in the sight of the Lord. Second Kings 21 tells the story of his atrocities. He rebuilt the high places (places of idol worship) which his father had destroyed and erected altars for Baal and Asherah. He even built altars for idols within the courts of the temple! But that's not all. He made his son pass through the fire (a method of sacrifice), practiced witchcraft, used divination, and dealt with mediums and spiritists. The Scripture says that he went so far as to do more evil than the pagan nations the Hebrews had driven out of Canaan.

Now you think someone like Manasseh would know better. Though he might not know of Moses' warning in Deuteronomy 4:25-27 which says, "When you become the father of children and children's children and have remained long in the land, and act corruptly, and make an idol in the form of anything, and do that which is evil in the sight of the LORD your God so as to provoke him to anger, I call heaven and earth to witness against you today, that you will surely perish quickly from the land where you are going over the Jordan to possess it. You shall not live long on it, but shall be utterly destroyed. The LORD will *scatter* you among the peoples, and you will be left few in number among the nations, where the LORD drives you;" yet, Manasseh definitely would remember that God divided the kingdom because Solomon did something similar. He also would recall that during his father's reign that God used the Assyrians to destroy the northern kingdom because Israel had worshipped created gods. Unfortunately, he deliberately chose to disobey the Creator God. The son of the godliest king of Judah becomes known as the wickedest king of Judah.

In response to this wickedness, God declares (2 Kings 24:3) that He will deliver the southern kingdom of Judah over to her enemies. And He does. Within forty years God uses the Babylonian nation to conquer Judah and take her into captivity. Scripture often calls this **exiling of Judah** a scattering from which we get our name for this seventh era, the Scattered Era. The italicized word in the preceding paragraph which was added for emphasis shows just one example of Scripture using the same word.

Before delving into how Babylon scatters Judah, take a look at the chart on page 13 to see which books fall within this era. Notice only two chapters (not books) detail the historical events. Another chapter, 2 Chronicles 36 adds the color commentary. The prophetical books of Daniel and Ezekiel complete the Scripture devoted to the Scattered Era.

HOW?

We found the United Era contains three kings (Saul, David, and Solomon) and the Divided Era three kingdoms (Israel, Judah, and Assyria).

So how can we remember what happens during the Scattered Era? We can recall the key events of this current era by realizing that Judah's exile took place in stages. The people of God left their Promised Land for Babylon in **three departures**. Each departure occurs under one of the last three kings of Judah. Let's pick up the story at the end of 2 Kings 23 in order to understand the broader context of what was going on in the world as the Scattered Era begins.

In verses 28 and 29 we discover a big war developing. Egypt has allied itself with Assyria to battle a new threatening power. Though not clear until the next chapter, 2 Kings 24, this new power is Babylon. Judah's king sees the danger posed to his own country. If Egypt and Assyria win, it would result in Egypt surrounding his small country. To avoid this trap he attempts to turn Egypt away by fighting from a well-fortified defensive position. If successful, then Assyria would have to fight Babylon alone. The desired outcome would result in both countries being extremely weakened and thus eliminating both the ancient Assyrian threat and the growing Babylonian threat.

Unfortunately, the plan of the king of Judah didn't work. The Egyptian army killed him, demanded Judah pay tribute, and made one of the king's sons, Eliakim, the new king. Following a custom of that day to show his dominance over the new king, the Pharaoh changed Eliakim's name to Jehoiakim, the eighteenth king of Judah. We now enter the Scattered Era which we find in 2 Kings 24–25.

After defeating both Assyria and Egypt, Babylon now stands as undisputed ruler of that part of the world. As such, Jehoiakim must now submit to Babylon. He does so for three years and then rebels. The king of Babylon, Nebuchadnezzar, comes to Jerusalem to restore order. After besieging the royal city, he overcomes the rebellion and in retribution carries off the king and others in what we call the *first departure*. Among those he deports we find (from the book of Daniel 1:1–7) Daniel who becomes a prophet, as well as Shadrach, Meshach, and Abednego, the three who survive being thrown into a fiery furnace.

Nebuchadnezzar eventually allows Jehoiakim to return to Jerusalem according to Jeremiah 22:18–19. There Jehoiakim apparently instigates another rebellion forcing Nebuchadnezzar to once again send his army and place Jerusalem under siege. Before the end of the siege, however, Jehoiakim dies and his son Jehoiachin becomes king in his place.

Realizing the hopelessness of his situation and probably thinking he could remain a vassal king since it was his father who rebelled, this nineteenth sovereign of Judah surrenders to the Babylonian king. In an effort to discourage any future revolts, Nebuchadnezzar exiles anyone who could pose danger to his rule over Judah including Jehoiachin, government officials, military officers, and the craftsmen who made the instruments of war. The total number of those who left during this *second departure* equals ten thousand people. As 2 Kings 24:14 says, "None remained except the poorest people of the land."

Before returning to Babylon, Nebuchadnezzar chooses Mattaniah to serve as the twentieth, and what would become the final, king of Judah. Just as the Pharaoh had changed Jehoiakim's name to show his superiority, Nebuchadnezzar changed Mattaniah's name to Zedekiah.

Not wise enough to learn from the previous two kings, Zedekiah soon rebels against Nebuchadnezzar. By the beginning of 2 Kings 25 we find Nebuchadnezzar returning one last time to Judah where he besieges Jerusalem. The siege causes such a severe famine that the people eat their children in order to survive which Moses had predicted in Deuteronomy 28:49, 53, 64. (Also see Lamentations 4:10.)

The Babylonians finally breach the defensive city walls after a year and a half. With defeat imminent Zedekiah seeks to escape with some of his army. Captured near Jericho, the Babylonians take the king of Judah to the great Babylonian king. Nebuchadnezzar sentences Zedekiah to watch as the conquering soldiers slaughter his children. Then they blind Zedekiah, bind him with chains, and take him to Babylon.

DEPARTURE	SCRIPTURE	KING	WHO	WHY
FIRST	2 Kgs 24:1-7 2 Chron 36:4-8 Dan 1:1-7	Jehoiakim	Jehoiakim, part of royal family, and some noble youths (including Daniel, Shadrach, Meshach, and Abednego)	Jehoiakim rebelled against King Nebuchadnezzar
SECOND	2 Kgs 24:8-16 2 Chron 36:9-10 Ezk 1:1-2	Jehoiachin	Jehoiachin and his family, government officials, military officers, craftsmen, and Ezekiel	Jehoiakim instigated another revolt upon his return
THIRD	2 Kgs 24:17–25:17 2 Chron 36:11-21	Zedekiah	The rest of the people, leaving only the very poor	Zedekiah rebelled against Nebuchadnezzar

Nebuchadnezzar wasn't finished taking vengeance on his rebellious domain. He sent the captain of his guard to Jerusalem where he burned all the houses of the city including the four hundred-year-old temple and the king's palace. Then they destroyed what remained of the city walls so Jerusalem could no longer protect itself. Finally, he carried off into exile all the people leaving only some farmers to keep the country from becoming totally uninhabitable. This *third and final departure* also includes all the temple's valuable articles. Nothing remains of the nation's glorious past under Kings David and Solomon.

NEBUCHADNEZZAR'S THIRD INVASION	
Demolished the temple	2 Kings 25:9
Destroyed the walls	2 Kings 25:10
Deported the people	2 Kings 25:11

Why did God allow this to happen to His people? Second Chronicles 36:15-16 notes, "The LORD, the God of their fathers, sent word to them again and again by His messengers, because He had compassion on His people and on His dwelling place; but they continually mocked the messengers of God, despised His words and scoffed at His prophets, until the wrath of the LORD arose against His people, until there was no remedy."

In other words God had warned them that if they did not worship Him and Him alone that He would discipline them. They didn't, choosing instead to follow the sins of Manasseh so God kept His promise. Fortunately, when we get to the next era, we find God keeping another promise: that after seventy years He would allow them to return to the Promised Land. (See 2 Chronicles 36:21, Jeremiah 25:11–12; 29:10, and Daniel 9:2.)

WHERE?

The Scattered Era focuses on two places, Judah and **Babylon**. Tradition claims the city of Babylon stood on the traditional site of Babel established by Nimrod making it at the time the oldest city in existence. Once Babylon defeated Assyria it became the capital of a world power which Habakkuk predicted in chapter 1, verses 5–6. Nebuchadnezzar fortified the city with seventeen miles of double walls. It also boasted one of the seven wonders of the ancient world with its amazing hanging gardens. Today one finds the ruins of the city of Babylon fifty miles south of Baghdad in Iraq.

The map below shows the extent of Nebuchadnezzar's Babylonian empire.

The Babylonian Empire
606-538 BC

The map on the following page puts into perspective both the Babylonian captivity of this era as well as the exile of Israel under Assyria during the previous era.

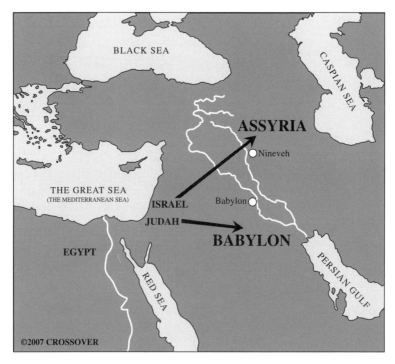

WHEN?

This seventh era begins in 605 BC with Nebuchadnezzar's first deportation of the people of Judah which included King Jehoiakim and Daniel, the noble youth who grew up to become a prophet. The era ends in 538 BC when God allows His people to return to Jerusalem under Zerubbabel whom we shall meet in the next era.

DEPARTURE	KING	WHEN
FIRST	Jehoiakim	605 BC
SECOND	Jehoiachin	597 BC
THIRD	Zedekiah	586 BC

Dating the Scattered Era from **605 to 538 BC** seems confusing because it overlaps by almost twenty years the Divided Era which lasted from 931 to 586 BC. What causes this overlap? To understand you must remember that this era contains three departures. The first departure of the people of Judah began their scattering, but did not end their kingdom. Not until the third departure did the reign of the last king of Judah come to an end.

	ISRAEL (10 Tribes)	JUDAH (2 Tribes)
ENDING DATE OF KINGDOM	722 BC	586 BC
DURATION OF KINGDOM	209 years	345 years
CONQUERER OF KINGDOM	Assyria	Babylon
DOWNFALL OF KINGDOM	Worshipping the golden calves	Walking in the sins of Manasseh

If we make the ending date of the Divided Era the same as the starting date for the Scattered Era (either 605 BC or 586 BC), we fail to communicate the actual date of either the end of the final king or the beginning of the first departure. For that reason we have the twenty year overlap.

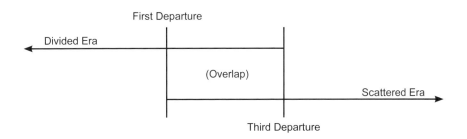

WHO?

Few people recognize the names of the three kings who ruled at the beginning of the Scattered Era: Jehoiakim, Jehoiachin, or even Zedekiah. Many people, however, recognize the name of **Daniel**, the young noble youth whom Nebuchadnezzar carried to Babylon during the first departure. Though he grew into a powerful government official in his foreign home, second only to the king, and also became a very powerful prophet, most people remember him for being thrown into the lions' den. Unfortunately, few can recall who threw him there or know why he did so.

The answers come from the sixth chapter of Daniel which tells the story of this godly man's uncompromising obedience to God. The chapter opens with King Darius of Persia about to promote Daniel over his entire kingdom, above all the other government officials. The king's decision provokes a power struggle. A cabal of officials looks for evidence of corruption to discredit Daniel. Finding none, they convince the king to issue a decree proclaiming no one could pray for thirty days to anyone but the king making the lions' den the penalty for disobedience. They figured correctly that this would get Daniel in trouble.

Read verse 10. What did Daniel do after the king signed the decree?

_____

_____

How quickly did he do this? _____

_____

How discreet did he try to be about what he was doing? _____

_____

Daniel's opponents obviously watch him closely to see what he would do. Little time lapses before they tell the king of Daniel's practice, even detailing how many times he kneels before his God. This information grieves the king, but he knows he must uphold the law so he has Daniel thrown into the lions' den.

The next morning the king hurries to the den to check on Daniel. In verse 20, the king asks Daniel a question that contains many clues about Daniel's commitment to God. How did the king describe Daniel's walk with God?

_____

_____

To King Darius' relief the lions have not injured Daniel in any way at all. This motivates the king to take two actions. First he has the malicious conspirators, their wives, and their children thrown into the lions' den where they meet an instant death. Second, he writes another decree. (Decrees were obviously big back then.) Read verses 25–27.

What did the king tell his people in verse 26 that they had to now do?

_____

_____

How did he describe God in verses 26 and 27?

_____

_____

To whom did he write this beautiful description of God? See verse 25.

_____

_____

_____

Daniel's uncompromising obedience resulted in the name of the living God being proclaimed to people of many different languages. Often when we read or hear the story of Daniel and the lions' den, we focus so intently on the miracle of Daniel's physical survival that we miss the greater point, the spiritual survival of untold numbers of people groups.

Since the beginning of the Nothing Era we have seen God's heart, not just for the Hebrew race, but for the human race. He wants to deliver (see verse 27) people from the spiritual penalty of their disobedience and reconcile them to Himself through the coming Messiah. Without knowing of God, how could they trust Him to deliver them? The king's proclamation as a result of Daniel's uncompromising obedience made sure that they knew.

Put yourself in Daniel's situation. Would you have continued to follow after God if you knew the king would throw you in the lions' den if you did? Would you follow God as openly as Daniel? (Remember he prayed three times a day with the windows open. He wanted people to know his ultimate loyalty.) If we honestly answer these questions, most of us would say "no." Yet, in our hearts we long to walk with God like Daniel. So how do we become men and women of no compromise? We grow in our commitment to God by obeying Him right now in the little things. Again, Daniel shows us how to do this.

Turn to chapter one of the book of Daniel. Here we find him as a youth having just arrived in Babylon from Judah. Because of their unique God-given abilities, Nebuchadnezzar's chief of staff chooses him and his three friends (whom we know by their Babylonian names as Shadrach, Meshach, and Abednego) to train them for service in the Babylonian government. We pick up the story in verse 8.

Daniel and his friends want to obey God. Yet, eating the meals of their captors would cause them to disobey Him since the Babylonians customarily sacrificed some of their food to their gods before eating it themselves. God had demonstrated in Exodus 34:15 that eating food sacrificed to idols displeased Him. Now this particular law of God does not rank as one of the most important commandments in the book of Exodus. It definitely did not make the Ten Commandments. What would it hurt for Daniel and his friends to compromise it? Certainly people would understand if as captives they adjusted to the cultural demands of their new environment.

Yet, Daniel did not think that way. He wanted to obey God even in the little things. Read Daniel 1:8. What did Daniel do?

_____

_____

Read verses 9–16. How did things turn out? _____

_____

Seeking to obey God in the small ways prepared Daniel for when it counted. Not only did this attitude of no compromise prepare Daniel, but it also prepared Daniel's friends. Turn to one last passage in this book, Daniel 3. In this chapter Nebuchadnezzar erects a golden image of himself and demands everyone must bow down before it to worship him. To maximize participation, the king declared he would burn alive all who disobeyed. This creative step would certainly increase church attendance for most of us, but not for Shadrach, Meshach, and Abednego. They refuse to compromise their commitment to God.

Nebuchadnezzar learns of the refusal of these three Jews. (During the Scattered Era the Hebrews become known as Jews, a shortened form of Judeans as in the people of Judah.) Enraged, he summons them to come to him and gives them a choice. Read verse 15. What is it?

_____

_____

How do they respond in verses 16–18? _____

_____

What an awesome response! Having learned obedience in the little things, they knew what to do in this situation. They chose to obey God regardless of the consequences. They had grown to possess an uncompromising commitment to God. Nebuchadnezzar, not being accustomed to anyone challenging his authority, orders the furnace heated seven times hotter than usual (apparently it got used fairly often) and for Daniel's three friends to be thrown inside.

Read verses 24–27. What does God do that surprises everyone?

_____

_____

_____

What happens greatly impacts Nebuchadnezzar. He proclaims in verse 28 that Shadrach, Meshach, and Abednego willingly yielded up their bodies so as not to serve or worship any god except their own God. That kind of commitment gets people's attention, even the most powerful people in the world.

As a result, Nebuchadnezzar issues, you probably guessed it, a decree. Read verse 29. What does he write in his decree and how many different people groups hear about the God of these three men of no compromise?

_____

_____

_____

God can use you in the lives of others as He did Daniel, Shadrach, Meshach, and Abednego, but you need to commit yourself to a life of no compromise. Is there any area of compromise in your life with which you need to deal today? If God has shown you something, do not hesitate to make it right before God and man regardless of how big or little it may be.

Though we've covered a lot, hopefully we've learned a lot about growing in our obedience to God. Let's articulate some of the main lessons we learned from Daniel and his friends.

Lesson 1 – We grow in our commitment to God by obeying God in the little things.

Lesson 2 – We should obey God openly, in front of our family, friends, and work associates.

Lesson 3 – Obeying God as He both desires and deserves has consequences. God sometimes delivers us. Yet, when He doesn't, He comforts us with His presence.

Lesson 4 – Kings like to issue decrees. (Just joking!) Uncompromising obedience to God gets the attention of unbelievers.

Lesson 5 – When unbelievers take notice that we Christians actually practice in our daily lives what we say we believe, then they will tell others about us. Though this does not excuse us from telling people about the Messiah, it does provide us with credibility when we do communicate the message of Christ.

What other lessons can you add from this week's reading?

_____

_____

_____

First Peter 3:15 says, "But sanctify Christ as Lord in your hearts, always being ready to make a defense to everyone who asks you to give an account for the hope that is in you, yet with gentleness and reverence." Let us make and keep Jesus Christ as Lord in our hearts, obeying Him always with uncompromising commitment. As we do, may many see our love for Christ and hear how they too can be reconciled to God.

We can now add to our spiritual growth chart.

FOUR AREAS OF SPIRITUAL GROWTH	IMPROPER STEPS	PROPER STEPS
Fellowship with God	Era 1 – Hiding our sin from God or blaming it on others.	Era 5 – Confessing our sin honestly and immediately to God.
Trust in God	Era 2 – Allowing fear to paralyze us.	Era 6 – Making prayer our first choice, not our last chance.
Obedience to God	Era 3 – Failing to follow-through on what God has commanded us to do.	Era 7 – Obeying God instantly regardless of the consequences.
Hearing from God	Era 4 – Thinking that simply knowing Scripture is enough to be spiritually mature.	Era 8 –

WHY?

The last two eras provided two very powerful Old Testament passages that point to the coming Messiah. Psalm 22 vividly describes *how* Christ would die (by the piercing of His hands and feet) and Isaiah 53 clearly details *why* Christ would die (in order to restore fellowship between all of us and Himself). The Scattered Era adds to these verses by identifying ***when Christ would die***.

The prophet Daniel (keep in mind that he lived during the Scattered Era) prophesies the timing of Christ's sacrifice in chapter 9, verse 25, of the book that bears his name, "So you are to know and discern that from the issuing of a decree to restore and rebuild Jerusalem until Messiah the Prince there will be seven weeks and sixty-two weeks." To better understand this verse, let's divide it up into its parts: the issuing of the decree to rebuild Jerusalem, the coming of the Messiah the Prince, and the seven and sixty-two weeks. Let's start with the decree to rebuild Jerusalem.

Scripture mentions four different decrees that relate to Jerusalem. The first two decrees made by King Cyrus and King Darius give the people of Judah permission to rebuild the temple or as the Scriptures say, the house of God. The third decree by King Artaxerxes provides money for the animals sacrificed inside the temple. None of these decrees, however, refer to the rebuilding of the city. Besides, a rebuilt temple within an unwalled city posed no threat to these kings.

The fourth decree, on the other hand, made by Artaxerxes in Nehemiah 2:1–8 does deal with the rebuilding of Jerusalem. It makes provision for Nehemiah to return from exile to rebuild the city's walls. (We will learn more about this in the next era.) So the decree mentioned in Daniel 9:25 refers to this fourth decree which Artaxerxes made in 444 BC.

KING	YEAR	DECREE	SCRIPTURE
Cyrus	538 BC	To rebuild the House of God	2 Chron 36:22-23 Ezra 1:1-4 Ezra 5:13
Darius I	520 BC	To confirm the previous decree	Ezra 6:1, 6-12
Artaxerxes	457 BC	To finance the sacrifices within the rebuilt temple	Ezra 7:11-26
Artaxerxes	444 BC	To rebuild the walls of Jerusalem	Nehemiah 2:1-8

Daniel's prophecy points to the coming of the Messiah. The time in between the decree to rebuild Jerusalem and the coming of the Messiah measures seven weeks plus sixty-two weeks for a total of sixty-nine weeks. (The word translated *weeks* in most Bibles actually means sevens, and most Bible scholars believe that in this prophecy the word stands for a period of years.) Let's see how close that comes to the most common dates for Christ's crucifixion, 30 AD and 33 AD.

If we multiply 69 times 7 we get 483 years. Adding this to 444 BC gives us a date of 39 AD. Close considering Daniel made the prophecy almost five hundred years earlier. But we have made a big mistake in our calculations.

Today we use the Gregorian calendar which contains 365 days a year. The calendar used by the people of Judah during the Scattered Era contained only 360 days per year. So we need to subtract 2415 days (483 years times 5 days per year). That many days equals over six and a half years. Now if we subtract 6 ½ years from 39 AD we get 32 AD.

You've got to admit, that's extremely close to the two most accepted years for dating when Christ died. Before we leave this "Why" section, answer this question. Do you remember from the Something Era the reason as to why God wanted to bless Abraham? God chose the Hebrews to bless them *so that* they might be a blessing to all the nations (or as some translations say, families) of the earth by proclaiming the Good News of the coming Messiah.

Now you may have forgotten the "so that," but Daniel didn't. In light of dating when the Messiah would come to die, look at what he writes in Daniel 7:14 about the coming Christ. The italics were added for emphasis. "And to Him was given dominion, glory and a kingdom, (so) that *all the peoples, nations, and men of every language* might serve Him." Even though many followers of God in the Old Testament forgot the "so that," we find some in every era who realized God desired fellowship with people from every ethnic group. Never did a time exist where He wanted fellowship with the Hebrews to the exclusion of everyone else.

A LITTLE EXTRA

You may have noticed above that a Babylonian king (Nebuchadnezzar) carried Daniel off into exile, but a Persian ruler (Darius the Mede) threw him into a lions' den. This confuses a lot of people. Understanding a bit of world history during that time clears up the matter. Not long after Babylon conquered the Assyrians in 612 BC and the Egyptians in 605 BC, the Persians conquered the Babylonians in 539 BC. This victory made Persia the fourth major empire that the Old Testament mentions.

By the time the New Testament begins we find the Roman Empire in power. In between the Persian and Roman Empires we find the Greeks reigning. Old Testament history, however, does not mention the Greeks or the Romans since Nehemiah wrote the last Old Testament book before these two came into power.

THE SIX OLD TESTAMENT EMPIRES

EMPIRE	ERA REIGNED
Egyptian	2, 3, 4, 5, 6
Assyrian	6
Babylonian	7
Persian	7, 8
Greek	8
Roman	8

The above chart helps us understand which empire reigned during each Old Testament era in the regions surrounding the Promised Land. The following maps detail the extent to which the final three empires reached.

The Persian Empire

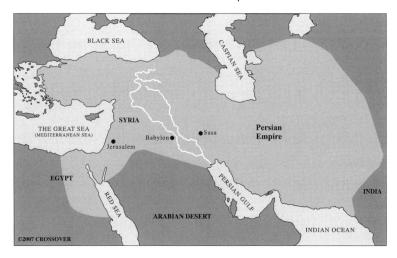

The Greek Empire

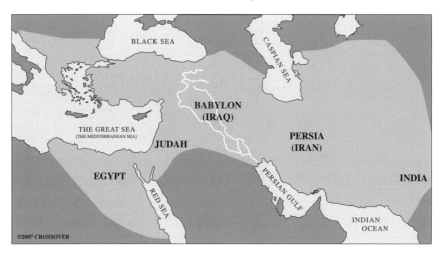

The Roman Empire

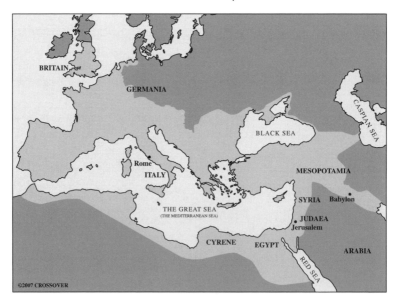

PUTTING TOGETHER THE PUZZLE OF THE OLD TESTAMENT

	OPTION 1 "An extremely busy week"	OPTION 2 "A little extra time"	OPTION 3 "Can't get enough"
DO	Next chapter – Era 8	Next chapter – Era 8	Next chapter – Era 8
READ		Average Readers: Read Ezra about how the people of God returned to their Promised Land Fast Readers: Add Nehemiah about how Jerusalem's walls were rebuilt Speed Readers: Add Esther about how God protected His people during their exile	Average Readers: Read Ezra about how the people of God returned to their Promised Land Fast Readers: Add Nehemiah about how Jerusalem's walls were rebuilt Speed Readers: Add Esther about how God protected His people during their exile
MEMORIZE (Choose one)			Seventh Era verse: Daniel 3:17-18 Seventh application verse: 2 Kings 24:3 Seventh Christ verse: Daniel 9:25 Seventh personal verse: choose your own

JUST FOR LAUGHS

A Sunday School teacher instructed her class to write a letter to God when they got home and to bring it back the following Sunday so they could read it to the class. Little Johnny wrote, "Dear God, we had a good time at church today. Wish you could have been there."

* * *

One summer evening during a violent thunderstorm, little Johnny's mother was tucking him in bed. She was about to turn off the light when he asked with a tremor in his voice, "Mommy, will you sleep in here with me tonight?" The mother smiled and gave Johnny a reassuring hug. "I can't, dear. I have to sleep in Daddy's room." A long silence was at last broken by his shaky little voice, "The big sissy!"

ERA #8

ERA #8

GATHERED JUDAH

(EZRA—NEHEMIAH)

We made it to the last era! Note, however, that we will review one last time in the next chapter since we will go over all eight eras. Making ourselves recall what we have studied lodges the information in our long-term memories and makes sure we retain the important issues found in each historical period of the Old Testament. So in the chart below fill in the items associated with the seven eras we have surveyed thus far. For Era #7 write the names of the kings associated with each of the three Babylonian departures. Writing the names will help familiarize you with these unusual monikers.

ERA #1	ERA #2	ERA #3	ERA #4
THE HUMAN RACE OUT OF _____	THE HEBREW RACE INTO _____	_____ EGYPT	_____ CANAAN

ERA #5	ERA #6	ERA #7
_____ KINGS STAND	_____ KINGS FALL	_____ JUDAH

As we have proceeded through each era, we have tried to grasp more than just what God did and how He did it. We sought to know why He did it. We discovered that the creator God made people for fellowship with Himself. When man's disobedience damaged that fellowship, God announced that He would send a Messiah to deliver the human race, not just the Hebrew race. Each era progressively revealed more and more about the coming Christ. What have the last three eras revealed about Christ?

ERA	#5	#6	#7
REVEALS	_____ Christ would die	_____ Christ would die	_____ Christ would die
SCRIPTURE	Psalm 22	Isaiah 53:4–6	Daniel 9:25

Most everyone familiar with the Bible knows that the New Testament stresses God reaching out to all people groups. Yet, we have clearly seen that this same theme runs through the Old Testament as well. As we properly assemble the various pieces of the Old Testament puzzle, the picture of God receiving glory by restoring fellowship between all people and Himself through His Son, Jesus Christ, comes more and more into focus.

Now let's see what this last era adds to the frame of our puzzle.

WHAT?

We ended the last era on a depressing note. During Nebuchadnezzar's final invasion he burned the temple, took away all but the poorest of Judah's people, and eliminated the future defense of Jerusalem by tearing down the city walls. The chart below from the last chapter summarizes the tragic circumstances of Judah.

NEBUCHADNEZZAR'S THIRD INVASION	
Demolished the temple	2 Kings 25:9
Destroyed the walls	2 Kings 25:10
Deported the people	2 Kings 25:11

God, however, never forgot His people. If in the last era He scattered them for their disobedience, in this era He orchestrates a **returning of Judah** because of His faithfulness. Not only does He gather the exiles, giving this era the name the Gathered Era, but also He orchestrates the rebuilding of the temple and the city walls. We will observe how this miraculously happens in the following section.

Before doing so, let's identify the six Old Testament books that belong to the Gathered Era. Two of the six, Ezra and Nehemiah, add directly to the historical flow of the biblical account of God restoring fellowship between man and Himself through the coming Messiah. The book of Esther, which falls during the time period that occurs between the sixth and seventh chapters of Ezra, adds color commentary. The other three books, Haggai, Zechariah, and Malachi, record the messages of these three prophets to the people of God during this time period.

HOW?

In much the same way the people of Judah left their Promised Land for Babylon in three departures, God gathers them in **three returns**. Each return, led by a specific leader of Judah, focuses on a specific task.

The *first return* occurs when King Cyrus, the Persian king who conquered the Babylonians and who threw the prophet Daniel into the lions' den, issues a decree declaring that the people of Judah could return to Jerusalem. Several reasons exist as to why he may have done this. Strategically, he wanted to build strong, loyal buffer states around the core of his kingdom. Yet, a deeper more spiritual reason exists. The prophet Jeremiah had predicted in Jeremiah 29:10 that the captivity would last only seventy years and Daniel knew this prophecy. (See Daniel 9:2.)

Do you recall from the last chapter the close relationship that, in spite of the little misunderstanding about the lions' den episode, Daniel had with the Persian kings? Perhaps Daniel used this connection to show King Cyrus (who followed King Darius) a very powerful prophecy. The prophet Isaiah, writing two centuries before the birth of Cyrus, had accurately foretold his name and his future undertaking saying, "It is I [the Lord] who says of Cyrus, 'He is My shepherd! And he will perform all My desire.' And he declares of Jerusalem, 'She will be built,' and of the temple, 'Your foundation will be laid'" (Isaiah 44:28). No wonder Cyrus confidently announces in Ezra 1:2 that the God of heaven had appointed him to build Him a house in Jerusalem.

Do not mistakenly think that after Cyrus issued the decree that the Jews living in captivity made a mad rush to return to their Promised Land. According to Ezra chapter 2, less than fifty thousand actually made the almost nine hundred mile trip. If we think about it, this makes sense. Though captives, they freely operated in the Persian society. Why leave a comfortable lifestyle and make a dangerous journey to a city in ruins? For some the reason was quite obvious. They longed to return to the site of the glorious temple and once again offer sacrifices as they worshipped the God of Heaven.

Zerubbabel, grandson of King Jehoiachin, leads the group in this first return to Jerusalem. Once there, according to Ezra chapter 3, he begins reconstruction on the temple. Unfortunately, Zerubbabel only finishes the foundation to the temple because the enemies of Judah using political connections bring a halt to the process for about fifteen years.

By Ezra chapter 5 the prophets Haggai and Zechariah arrive and encourage Zerubbabel to get started again on the temple. In spite of more opposition, they finish building the temple in Ezra chapter 6. After noting the dedication of the temple the Scripture next fittingly makes mention of the priests sacrificing the Passover lamb. The coming Messiah once again comes into focus.

RETURN	SCRIPTURE	WHO	WHAT	HOW
FIRST	The book of Ezra (Chapters 1-6)	Zerubbabel	Reconstructs the temple	Kings Cyrus and Darius issue decrees
SECOND	The book of Ezra (Chapters 7-10)	Ezra	Renews the people	King Artaxerxes issues a decree
THIRD	The book of Nehemiah	Nehemiah	Rebuilds the city walls	King Artaxerxes issues a decree

It takes almost sixty years after the completion of the temple before the *second return* to Jerusalem occurs. At this time Ezra, both a priest and a scribe, requests permission from Artaxerxes in Ezra chapter 7 to take money from Babylon to Jerusalem in order to buy sacrificial animals for the temple. The Persian king grants his permission and another group of less than two thousand people return.

Before leaving, Ezra proclaims a fast asking God to protect the group since they needed to travel hundreds of miles carrying all that money as well as all their possessions and loved ones. Though Ezra could have asked the king for troops to protect them on the journey, out of shame he did not ask the king since he had told Artaxerxes, "The hand of our God is favorably disposed to all those who seek Him, but His power and His anger are against all those who forsake Him." God demonstrated His faithfulness and the entire entourage arrived safely.

Once in Jerusalem Ezra finds the Jerusalem Jews in a sad spiritual state. The people of Judah, including the priests, had forsaken the commandments of God. One particularly grievous offense concerned their marriages with the Canaanite people groups who worshipped other gods. (You would think that they would have learned from the mistakes their forefathers made, but they didn't.) Ezra, so broken hearted that he pulls hair from his head and beard, falls to his knees in prayer before the temple.

As he confesses the disobedience of the nation of Israel, a large crowd gathers and begins to weep bitterly. Convicted of their sin, the people repent of their compromising lifestyles resulting in renewed spiritual commitment.

During the first return Zerubbabel reconstructs the demolished temple and during the second return Ezra renews the people. Only the rebuilding of the walls to protect the defenseless city remains. Nehemiah accomplishes this during the *third return.*

RETURN	LEADER	PROPHET
FIRST	Zerubbabel	Haggai and Zechariah
SECOND	Ezra	
THIRD	Nehemiah	Malachi

In chapter 1 of the book that bears his name, Nehemiah hears news from one of his brothers of the disastrous condition of Jerusalem. This revelation causes Nehemiah to weep, mourn, pray, and fast for days. As he does so, he asks God (verses 8–9) to remember what He had said to Moses, "If you are unfaithful I will *scatter* you among the peoples; but if you return to Me and keep My commandments and do them, though those of you who have been *scattered* were in the most remote part of the heavens, I will *gather* them from there and will bring them to the place where I have chosen to cause

My name to dwell." (Read Leviticus 26:27, 33 and Deuteronomy 30:2–4, emphasis added.)

After reminding God of His promise both to scatter the unfaithful and to gather the obedient, Nehemiah asks God to make him successful before a certain man. We don't know this man's identity until the next chapter of Nehemiah. There we discover that Nehemiah serves as cupbearer to King Artaxerxes, the same king who allowed Ezra to return to Jerusalem.

Serving in such a role places Nehemiah in a position of great confidence to the king since it requires that he tastes the king's wine to protect him from being poisoned. Only someone in whom the king completely trusted could fill such an important position of responsibility. When Artaxerxes inquires why Nehemiah looks so sad, Nehemiah explains the condition of Jerusalem's walls and asks permission to do something about it.

Artaxerxes issues a decree permitting Nehemiah to return and rebuild the city walls. Unfortunately, Scripture does not mention how many exiles make the eleven hundred mile trip with him. Once in Jerusalem, Nehemiah overcomes opposition and rebuilds the walls in fifty-two days, less time than it took him to make the two month trip from Susa, the capitol of the Persian Empire.

Having cared for the physical needs of the people of Jerusalem, Nehemiah in the eighth chapter of the book that bears his name now turns his attention to the spiritual needs of the people. He teams up with Ezra who explains the Scripture to the people. (The prophet Malachi also ministers during this time.)

As they begin to hear and understand God's Word, the people weep, pray, and fast as they realize how much they have disobeyed God. In chapter nine of Nehemiah, they confess their sins and the sins of their forefathers. If you read through this chapter, notice that they mention all eight eras of Old Testament history. Notice also how they describe both God and themselves during each era. In chapter ten the people sign a covenant committing themselves to follow God and His Word whole-heartedly.

SCATTERED ERA	GATHERED ERA
Nebuchadnezzar demolishes the temple	Zerubbabel reconstructs the temple
Nebuchadnezzar deports the people	Ezra renews the people
Nebuchadnezzar destroys the walls	Nehemiah rebuilds the walls

With the closing of the book of Nehemiah, we come to an end of recorded Old Testament history. Another four centuries, however, remain before the ultimate Passover Lamb arrives to overcome sin and Satan through His death on the cross. Most Bible students call these four hundred years the "silent years" because we have no further biblical information written during this time.

Yet we know God has not forgotten the nations who desperately need spiritual deliverance. God was waiting on the fullness of time. Two future empires would soon make contributions that would allow God's people to communicate to the world that Jesus Christ the Messiah had finally come. The Greek Empire would provide a universal language and the Roman Empire would provide the Roman road system and peace (Pax Romana) allowing the Good News of Christ to cover the known world in a matter of decades.

WHERE?

The events of the Gathered Era basically occur in the same two places as the events of the Scattered Era, Babylon as well as Judah located in the land of **Canaan**. Recall, however, that the Persians (perhaps more accurately the Medes and Persians) ultimately conquer the Babylonians. The first two returns originate from the city of Babylon, the former capital of the Babylonians. The third return under Nehemiah leaves from Susa the capital of the Persians located east of Babylon.

The following map orients us to the location of Jerusalem within the Persian empire.

The Persian Empire

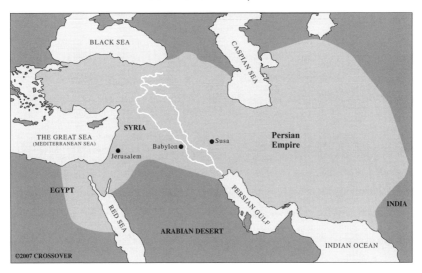

WHEN?

The Gathered Era begins in 538 BC when God allows for the first return of His people to Jerusalem under Zerubbabel. Two more returns subsequently leave for Jerusalem. The final return under Nehemiah however does not mark the end of this era. The Gathered Era comes to an end with the arrival of the Messiah in the New Testament. So we set the starting and ending dates for this era as **538 BC to the coming of Christ**.

RETURN	WHO	WHEN
FIRST	Zerubbabel	538 BC
SECOND	Ezra	458 BC
THIRD	Nehemiah	444 BC

One other important aspect about the timing of the Gathered Era needs mentioning before leaving this "When" section. Let's look more carefully at the prophecy of Jeremiah which predicted the people of Judah would remain in exile for a period of seventy years. We find it in the book that bears his name. Writing from Jerusalem and before the exile had occurred he pens, "For thus says the Lord, 'When seventy years have been completed for Babylon, I will visit you and fulfill My good word to you, to bring you back to this place'" (Jeremiah 29:10).

Here's our question: How close did he come with his prediction?

From the previous chapter we know that Nebuchadnezzar deported the first group from Jerusalem in 605 BC. We also learned above that Zerubbabel led the first return to Jerusalem in 538 BC to rebuild the temple. Counting the years *separating the people from their city* equals sixty-eight years. Not bad!

We must remember, however, that the house of God made the city of Jerusalem special. To the people of Judah, the temple represented fellowship with God with the offerings and feasts so closely associated with it. It served as the visible reminder of God's presence with them. Zerubbabel returned to Jerusalem to rebuild the temple, not just to live in the city. If we use the year he started reconstruction of the temple (536 BC) as the ending date, which the prophet may actually have had in mind, then we end up with 70.5 years *separating the people from their temple*. Jeremiah was right on target.

WHO?

It's much more fun pronouncing the name of Zerubbabel; and more people seem to recognize the name of Nehemiah than the name of **Ezra**. Yet in this section we want to examine the life of the latter in order to see what we can gain from his life to motivate our own spiritual growth. Specifically let's look at Ezra's commitment to the Scripture as seen in the seventh chapter of the book that bears his name.

Read Ezra 7:6, 11, 12, and 21. These four verses identify Ezra in a certain way. (Note: verses 11, 12, and 21 add a second role, but only one role is seen in all four verses.) What do they call him?

_____

_____

During the previous era, the Scattered Era, two institutions emerged that continued into the times of the New Testament. The first institution we know as the synagogue, a word which means "gathering" and consisted of at least ten Jewish males. Since the people did not have the temple as the center of worship with its sacrificial offerings and feasts, the people gathered together in small groups to study the Word of God on the Sabbath.

The second institution that developed in the Scattered Era we know as the Scribes (or teachers of the Law). From this point forward they play a significant role in biblical history. They begin the synagogue system, make copies of the Scriptures thus preserving them for posterity, and they interpret the law of God to others. Initially, their contribution is very positive, but in this latter role they eventually err. By New Testament times they have elevated their own interpretations above what the Scriptures actually say and become strong opponents of Christ.

Read Ezra 7:10. What three commitments did Ezra make in regards to the Scriptures?

_____

_____

_____

Let's look at each one of these three commitments beginning with the first one. Read verses 6 and 11. How well did Ezra know the Word of God?

_____

_____

_____

Ezra's example challenges us! To know the Bible to this degree takes effort, weekly if not daily. But it takes something else as well. With our busy lifestyles it also takes a plan. When you finish this study on the Old Testament what steps will you take to continue your study of Scripture? Specifically:

What do you plan to study? _____

What time each week or day will you set aside to study? _____

Where will you do your studying? _____

If you are going through this book as part of a group, you may need to consult them before making a decision. Hopefully having to think through these questions now will allow you to continue your Bible study without any unnecessary delays in between topics.

SCRIPTURE	EZRA'S COMMITMENT TO SCRIPTURE
Ezra 7:6	This Ezra . . . was a scribe skilled in the law of Moses.
Ezra 7:10	For Ezra had set his heart to study the law of the LORD, and to practice it, and to teach His statues and ordinances in Israel.
Ezra 7:11	Ezra the priest, the scribe, learned in the words of the commandments of the LORD and His statutes.

Ezra 7:12	Artaxerxes, king of kings, to Ezra the priest, the scribe of the law of the God of heaven.
Ezra 7:14	According to the law of your God which is in your hand.
Ezra 7:21	Ezra the priest, the scribe of the law of the God of heaven.
Ezra 7:25	Even all those who know the laws of your God; and you may teach anyone who is ignorant of them.
Nehemiah 8:1	They asked Ezra the scribe to bring the book of the law of Moses which the LORD had given to Israel.
Nehemiah 8:2	Then Ezra the priest brought the law before the assembly of men, women and all who could listen with understanding .
Nehemiah 8:3	He read from it . . . from early morning until midday, in the presence of men and women, those who could understand; and all the people were attentive to the book of the law.
Nehemiah 8:5	Ezra opened the book in the sight of all the people for he was standing above all the people; and when he opened it, all the people stood up.
Nehemiah 8:13	All the people . . . were gathered to Ezra the scribe that they might gain insight into the words of the law.
Nehemiah 8:18	He read from the book of the law of God daily, from the first day to the last day.

Let's look at the second commitment Ezra made in verse 10. The three commitments are arranged in a sequential order. What is the logic behind this arrangement? Would rearranging the three commitments make any sense? Why?

_____

_____

_____

Though a logical order of the three exists, an equal importance does not. Practicing God's Word is paramount. Teaching the Scriptures without practicing them makes us hypocrites. Studying the Scripture without practicing them makes us proud. Truly practicing what we study allows us to grow in Christ-like character and provides credibility when we teach. If you read Ezra 9:1 to 10:4 you will see both of these in the life of Ezra.

Review the spiritual growth chart on page 180. Which of the steps do you need to put into practice the most? Why?

_____

_____

_____

We now come to Ezra's third commitment. Life teaches that three stages of physical growth exist: as a baby others feed you, as a child you feed you, and as an adult you feed others. We see these same three stages, not only in the physical realm, but in the spiritual realm as well. As new or baby Christians we need others to feed us spiritually, teaching us about Christ and His Word. As we grow spiritually, we reach a point where we no longer need others to feed us because we have learned how to go to Scripture and feed ourselves. Perhaps one day we know enough about the Word of God that others ask us to teach them.

As a baby Christian	As a young Christian	As an older Christian
others feed you	you feed you	you feed others

Where did Ezra fall on this continuum?

_____

_____

Where do you fall on this continuum? Are you satisfied where you are? What can you do to change the status quo?

_____

_____

We find the key to all three of Ezra's commitments at the beginning of chapter seven verse ten. "Ezra had set his heart." As with most areas of spiritual growth, it all boils down to an issue of the heart.

Let's see what lessons we can learn from Ezra.

Lesson 1 – We can know Scripture if we make the time to study it.

Lesson 2 – Studying Scripture without practicing it leads to pride, whereas practicing what we study leads to Christ-like character or rather true spiritual maturity.

Lesson 3 – Teaching Scripture without practicing it makes us hypocrites.

Lesson 4 – Having a plan may make us more consistent at studying our Bibles.

Lesson 5 – We must examine our hearts to see how much we truly value the Word of God.

What other lessons can you add from this week's reading?

_____

_____

_____

Second Timothy 3:16–17 says, "All Scripture is inspired by God and profitable for teaching, for reproof, for correction, for training in righteousness; that the man of God may be adequate, equipped for every good work." May we set our hearts to study and practice and whenever possible teach the wonderful truths of God's Word.

We can finish adding the last step to our spiritual growth chart.

FOUR AREAS OF SPIRITUAL GROWTH	IMPROPER STEPS	PROPER STEPS
Fellowship with God	Era 1 – Hiding our sin from God or blaming it on others.	Era 5 – Confessing our sin honestly and immediately to God.
Trust in God	Era 2 – Allowing fear to paralyze us.	Era 6 – Making prayer our first choice, not our last chance.
Obedience to God	Era 3 – Failing to follow-through on what God has commanded us to do.	Era 7 – Obeying God instantly regardless of the consequences.
Hearing from God	Era 4 – Thinking that simply knowing Scripture is enough to be spiritually mature.	Era 8 – Setting our hearts to study and practice what the Word of God teaches.

WHY?

By now you probably realize the astonishing accuracy of biblical prophecy. Yet God has created some of us a bit more skeptical than others. In other words, some of us may think that any prophecy can be seen as accurate in retrospect. If we know how Christ died, then we search the Old Testament until we find a verse which talks about piercing and declare it predicts the coming Christ. By unscrupulously manipulating Scripture in this way, we can always "prove" the accuracy of biblical prophecy. Since this possibility exists, a nagging question lingers in our minds: Did the people of the Old Testament consider any verses prophecy?

Great question! Let's answer it by asking another question. What did Herod, king of the Jews at the birth of Christ, initially do when the wise men told him they had come to worship the newly born king of the Jews? You may want to refer to Matthew 2:1–6 in the New Testament. Verse 4 says he gathered all the chief priests and scribes and inquired as to where the Christ was to be born. They confidently replied, "In Bethlehem of Judea."

Now why did they answer Bethlehem? Easy, they had studied the Old Testament Scripture and knew certain verses contained prophecies of the coming Messiah. Paraphrasing Micah 5:2 they said, "And you, Bethlehem, land of Judah, are by no means least among the leaders of Judah; for out of you shall come forth a Ruler, who will shepherd My people Israel."

Hopefully it helps to see that the Jewish people identified certain Old Testament verses as prophecies of the coming Messiah *before* Christ ever arrived making it a bit easier for us to at least accept that such prophecies exist.

In the last three eras we saw Scripture foretelling *how*, *why*, and *when* Christ would die. During this era we find Scripture predicting *where* Christ would die.

Zechariah, one of the prophets who encouraged Zerubbabel while he rebuilt the temple, first sets the context of the days before Christ's death by proclaiming, "Rejoice greatly, O daughter of Zion! Shout in triumph, O daughter of Jerusalem! Behold, your king is coming to you; He is just and endowed with salvation, humble, and mounted on a donkey, even on a colt, the foal of a donkey" (Zechariah 9:9). Then he predicts, "I will pour out on the house of David and on the inhabitants of Jerusalem, the Spirit of grace and of supplication, so that they will look on Me whom they have pierced; and they will mourn for Him, as one mourns for an only son, and they will weep bitterly over Him like the bitter weeping over a firstborn" (Zechariah 12:10).

Zechariah identifies where Christ would die by prophesying that the Messiah would make a triumphal entry into Jerusalem (John 12:12–16) and that the inhabitants of Jerusalem would look on (John 19:37) as the nails pierced Jesus at His crucifixion.

Please do not allow the details regarding the how, why, when, and where of Christ's death to cloud the reason He came to die. Once again, the theme of Scripture including the Old Testament focuses on God receiving glory by restoring fellowship between the nations and Himself through the sacrifice of His Son, Jesus Christ. Zechariah places the spotlight on God's heart for all the peoples of the earth when he says, "Many nations will join themselves to the LORD in that day and will become My people. Then I will dwell in your midst, and you will know that the LORD of hosts has sent Me to you" (Zechariah 2:11).

A LITTLE EXTRA

Life for the people of God revolved around the temple, the visible expression of God's promise to dwell with them. For this reason Zerubbabel risking great dangers left Babylon during the Gathered Era in order that he might rebuild the temple in Jerusalem. Why then, except for what we find in the books of Ezra and Nehemiah, do we never read anything in the Bible about Zerubbabel's temple? We read about Solomon's temple in the Old Testament and about Herod's temple in the New Testament. Where did Zerubbabel's temple go?

Though damaged by invasions during the five hundred years between its construction and the time of Christ, Zerubbabel's temple did not disappear. Two reasons, however, exist why we don't read much about it in Scripture. First we don't read much about it in the Old Testament because Zerubbabel built it near the end of recorded Old Testament history. Four hundred of the

Herod's Temple

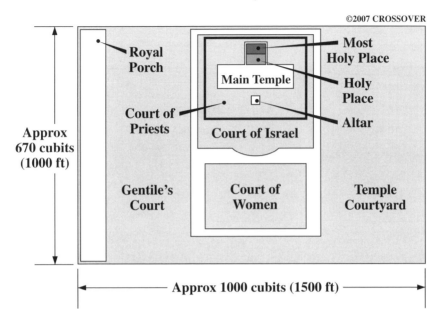

Approx 670 cubits (1000 ft)

Royal Porch

Most Holy Place

Main Temple

Holy Place

Court of Priests

Court of Israel

Altar

Gentile's Court

Court of Women

Temple Courtyard

Approx 1000 cubits (1500 ft)

five hundred years of its existence fall within the "silent years." (See the preceding "How" section.)

Second, we don't read about it at all in the New Testament because just before the birth of Christ, Herod the Great launched a major renovation of Zerubbabel's temple. So extensive was the construction that people referred to the result as Herod's temple. Unfortunately, the Romans destroyed the edifice in 70 AD.

FOR NEXT TIME

	OPTION 1 "An extremely busy week"	OPTION 2 "A little extra time"	OPTION 3 "Can't get enough"
DO	Next chapter – Conclusion	Next chapter – Conclusion	Next chapter – Conclusion
READ		Catch up on any reading you may have not finished.	Catch up on any reading you may have not finished.
MEMORIZE (Choose one)			Eighth Era verse: Nehemiah 1:9 Eighth application verse: Ezra 7:10 Eighth Christ verse: Zechariah 9:9 or 12:10 Eighth personal verse: choose your own

JUST FOR LAUGHS

The following list compiles conversations of children with God.

1. *Dear God, please put another holiday between Christmas and Easter. There is nothing good in there now. Amanda, age 5*

2. *Dear God, thank you for the baby brother, but what I asked for was a puppy. I never asked for anything before. You can look it up. Joyce, age 6*

3. *Dear Mr. God, I wish you would not make it so easy for people to come apart. I had to have 3 stitches and a shot. Janet, age 4*

4. *God, I read the Bible. What does beget mean? Nobody will tell me. Alison, age 6*

5. *Dear God, how did you know you were God? Who told you? Charlene, age 7*

6. *Dear God, is it true my father won't get in heaven if he uses his golf words in the house? Anita, age 8*

7. *Dear God, I bet it's very hard for you to love everybody in the whole world. There are only 4 people in our family and I can never do it. Nancy, age 7*

8. *Dear God, I like the story about Noah the best of all of them. You really make up some good ones. I like walking on water, too. Glenn, age 4*

9. *Dear God, my Grandpa says you were around when he was a little boy. How far back do you go? Dennis, age 5*

10. *Dear God, do you draw the lines around the countries? If you don't, who does? Nathan, age 7*

11. *Dear God, I am doing the best I can. Really. Frank, age 4*

12. *Dear God, I didn't think orange went with purple until I saw the sunset you made on Tuesday night. That was really cool. Thomas, age 6*

CONCLUSION

CONCLUSION

ADMIRING THE PUZZLE'S BORDER

Nine chapters ago we emptied out the box containing the pieces of the Old Testament puzzle. After studying the box cover we realized that when properly put together the puzzle produces a picture of God, specifically a picture of God receiving glory by restoring fellowship between the nations and Himself through His Son, Jesus Christ. Having made this discovery we searched for the corner pieces or categories which provided an organizational framework to begin assembling the puzzle. We found that each of the thirty-nine books of the Old Testament fall into one of three categories: historical, poetical, or prophetical.

We then focused on the historical category to find the straight-edged pieces. We determined that thirteen of the seventeen historical books systematically presented the biblical events that occurred from the creation of the world until the coming of the promised Messiah. These events divided into eight eras of Old Testament history. Within each of the time periods, we discovered three to four key items for a total of twenty-eight items. As we chapter by chapter connected these key items, we framed in the puzzle.

The effort spent paid off. We now understand what God did to prepare the nations for the coming Messiah. So for one last time, let's review the eight eras and the key items that they contain. Remember, under Era #8 you want to name the three men who led each of the three returns to Jerusalem.

ERA #1	ERA #2	ERA #3	ERA #4
THE HUMAN RACE OUT OF _____	THE HEBREW RACE INTO _____	_____ EGYPT	_____ CANAAN

ERA #5	ERA #6	ERA #7	ERA #8
_____ KINGS STAND	_____ KINGS FALL	_____ JUDAH	_____ JUDAH

As we conclude our efforts to better understand the puzzle of the Old Testament, we will continue with our format of answering six investigative questions. As we do, we will try to make some final connections in hope of gaining an even clearer understanding of what God did in preparation for the coming Christ.

WHAT?

We can now answer the question, "What was God doing in the Old Testament?" by explaining four pairs of opposite words: Nothing/Something, Exiting/Entering, United/Divided, and Scattered/Gathered. These combinations thoroughly but simply describe eight distinct eras of divine activity on earth.

HISTORICAL ERA	OLD TESTAMENT BOOK
Nothing	Genesis 1-11
Something	Genesis 12-50
Exiting	Exodus
Exiting	Leviticus
Exiting	Numbers
Exiting	Deuteronomy
Entering	Joshua
Entering	Judges
United	1 Samuel
United	2 Samuel
United	1 Kings 1-11
Divided	1 Kings 12-22
Divided	2 Kings 1-23
Scattered	2 Kings 24-25
Gathered	Ezra
Gathered	Nehemiah

Though we may easily remember the names of these eight eras, we may have lost perspective on where each occurred in Scripture. The above chart places each era in its proper biblical context. We included only the thirteen books which contribute to the historical flow of the Old Testament. We omitted Ruth, 1 Chronicles, 2 Chronicles, and Esther from the chart because they only added color commentary. Notice Genesis, 1 Kings, and 2 Kings each overlap two eras. Genesis covers both the Nothing and Something Eras, 1 Kings covers both the United and Divided Eras, and 2 Kings overlaps the Divided and Scattered Eras.

HOW?

Having reviewed the big picture, let's focus on the details. How did God specifically prepare the nations for the coming of Jesus Christ? The eight paragraphs below describe the story of the Old Testament using the twenty-eight key items learned in this book. To help you better identify the twenty-eight key items, we highlighted them in boldface italics.

In the Nothing Era the book of Genesis reveals that God creates the human race out of nothing. Four events summarize this first era. The *creation* of man begins with Adam and Eve walking in perfect fellowship with God. Unfortunately, Adam and Eve disobey God. As a consequence of the *fall* of man, God banishes them and their descendants from His presence making fellowship with Him impossible. He does not leave them without hope, however, and promises a coming Messiah who would deliver them from their disobedience and restore fellowship once again. As mankind multiplies, they become more and more wicked. In response God brings about the judgment of man by sending a *flood*. Only Noah and his family survive because of the ark which God provides. The era ends with man attempting to build the great *tower of Babel* to himself and not to God. The Lord stops the work by confusing everyone's language. This division of man separates the human race into various people or ethnic groups.

The Old Testament story continues by showing how God turns the Hebrew race into something of great size and significance. At the beginning of this second era God promises to give *Abraham* the land of Canaan. God also promises to use Abraham to bless the nations by sending the Messiah through his descendants. The rest of the book of Genesis traces God's dealings with Abraham's immediate descendants: *Isaac*, *Jacob*, and *Joseph*. Though the growth of this people group starts slowly through these four patriarchs, by the end of the Something Era they increase to a great multitude.

The third era opens in the land of Egypt. At this point in biblical history, the Egyptians have enslaved the Hebrews who had moved there in order to avoid a famine in the land of Canaan. The meanings of the titles of the next four books in the Old Testament tell the story of what happens in the Exiting Era. In the book of *Exodus* (which means to depart) the Hebrews depart from Egypt through the Red Sea to Mount Sinai where they receive the Ten Commandments. In the book of *Leviticus* (which means pertaining to the Levitical priests) God gives instructions on how to worship Him in the form of five offerings and seven feasts. In *Numbers* Moses counts the Hebrews and then leads them to the edge of the Promised Land. The people fear to enter and God makes them wander in the wilderness for their lack of faith. After this disobedient generation dies, Moses counts them for a second time as they prepare to enter the Promised Land. Finally, in *Deuteronomy* Moses gives the Ten Commandments for a second time so this new generation of Hebrews has the Law firmly fixed in their minds before possessing the land of Canaan.

During the Entering Era the Hebrews conquer the Canaanites physically, but the Canaanites conquer the Hebrews spiritually. In disobedience to the Ten Commandments the Hebrews *sin* by worshipping Baal and Asheroth, the gods of the Canaanites. To win them back, not to pay them back, the Creator God allows the Hebrews to experience *suffering*. When they come to their senses the Hebrews cry out to God. God answers their *supplication* and sends them a deliverer who brings them *salvation* from their physical bondage. Sadly, the Hebrews go through this cycle not once but six different times during this fourth era.

As the years go by, the Hebrews transition from a confederation of twelve loosely affiliated tribes into a monarchy. Three kings reign during this United Era. The Scripture characterizes *Saul*, the first of these kings, as not having a heart for God but for himself. Though *David* commits two horrible sins, Scripture considers this second king as a man after God's own heart because of his humble response to God after he sins. *Solomon*, the last of these three kings serves God with a half heart. He starts his rule with tremendous devotion toward God, but compromises near the end when he turns his heart to worship the gods of the Canaanites. During this era God reveals how the coming Messiah will die to pay the penalty for people's disobedience.

Three kingdoms describe the history of the Divided Era. As a consequence of Solomon worshipping other gods, God uses a rebellion to divide the nation of Israel into two separate kingdoms. The ten northern tribes form one kingdom and keep the name *Israel*, though sometimes Scripture refers to it as Ephraim. The two tribes located in the south form a second kingdom known as *Judah* after the larger of the two tribes. Israel, led by nineteen wicked kings, never follows after the Lord God but instead worships two golden calves. God uses a third kingdom, *Assyria*, to conquer Israel and relocate its people. These relocated tribes become known as the ten lost tribes of Israel. In this time period, God uses the prophet Isaiah to foretell why the coming Messiah must die.

Though more faithful than Israel, Judah does not always worship the Lord. The worst of Judah's twenty kings, Manasseh, sends Judah down a sinful path from which she never recovers. To teach them an invaluable lesson God allows Nebuchadnezzar of Babylon to conquer the people of Judah and to take them into exile for seventy years. The exile does not happen all at once but occurs in three departures, each one under one of the last three kings of Judah. Nebuchadnezzar takes king *Jehoiakim* and a few others including Daniel, Shadrach, Meshach, and Abednego during the first departure. In the second departure he deports king *Jehoiachin* and ten thousand captives. In the final departure Nebuchadnezzar carries off king **Zedekiah** and all but the poorest of the land. During this Scattered Era, Daniel predicts when the coming Messiah will die on behalf of the nations.

Faithful to His promise God allows the Babylonian exile to last only seventy years. Under the authority of Persian kings God sends His people back to Jerusalem. Three separate returns under three different leaders mark this Gathered Era. First **Zerubbabel** leads a group back to reconstruct the temple. Later **Ezra** leads a return to Jerusalem. There he reforms the spiritual lives of the people of Judah. **Nehemiah** leads the final return where he rebuilds the defensive city walls of Jerusalem. Zechariah, a prophet who labors with Zerubbabel, prophesies during this time as to where the future Christ will die.

The book of Nehemiah brings an end to the recorded history of the Old Testament. Yet four hundred years remain until the birth of Christ. During this time, called the silent years, God uses two kingdoms to make the final preparations for the coming Messiah. The Greek Empire spreads a universal language and the Roman Empire builds a universal road-system and oversees an unprecedented peace. The combination of these three factors will allow the Good News of God restoring fellowship between man and Himself through His Son, Jesus Christ, to spread quickly and safely to the nations.

WHERE?

In each individual era we located where the events primarily occurred. In this section we want to capture the general flow of all eight eras. The numbers on the following two maps correspond to the numbers in the following chart. From the chart you can then identify what happened at that particular location, where it occurred, and when it transpired.

Locations of Old Testament Events

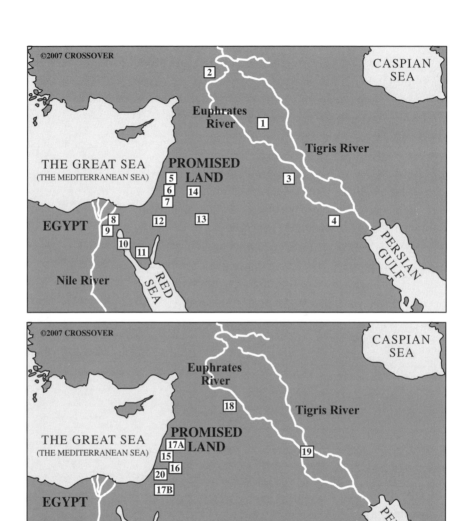

©2007 CROSSOVER

CASPIAN SEA

Euphrates River

Tigris River

THE GREAT SEA (THE MEDITERRANEAN SEA)

PROMISED LAND

EGYPT

Nile River

RED SEA

PERSIAN GULF

NUMBER	WHAT	WHERE	WHEN
1	Fall of man	Garden of Eden	Nothing Era
2	Judgment of man	Noah's Ark	Nothing Era
3	Division of man	Tower of Babel	Nothing Era
4	God calls Abraham to leave for a Promised Land	Ur	Something Era
5	Abraham arrives in Canaan	Canaan	Something Era
6	Isaac lives in Canaan	Canaan	Something Era
7	Jacob lives in Canaan	Canaan	Something Era
8	Joseph arrives in Egypt	Egypt	Something Era
9	Moses leads Hebrews out of Egypt	Egypt	Exiting Era
10	Moses leads Hebrews through the Red Sea	Red Sea	Exiting Era
11	Moses leads Hebrews to Mt. Sinai	Mount Sinai	Exiting Era
12	People refuse to enter Promised Land	Kadesh	Exiting Era
13	People wander in the wilderness	Wilderness	Exiting Era
14	People receive the Ten Commandments for a second time	Moab	Exiting Era
15	Joshua leads people into the Promised Land	Canaan	Entering Era
16	Saul, David, and Solomon rule a united kingdom	Nation of Israel	United Era
17	The nation divides into northern and southern kingdoms	17A Israel	Divided Era
		17B Judah	
18	Israel carried off by Assyria	Assyria	Divided Era
19	Judah exiled to Babylon	Babylon	Scattered Era
20	Judah returns to the Promised Land	Canaan	Gathered Era

Draw an arrow from location to location, starting with the number one. This exercise will help you better visualize the geographical movement of Old Testament events. (Note: Number 16 goes two different directions, to numbers 17A and 17 B. Number 17A terminates at number 18. Number 17B goes to number 19 which in turn terminates at number 20.

WHEN?

Many of us appreciate knowing when in history the Old Testament events occurred. Unfortunately, we cannot always recall but a few of the specific dates. If remembering numbers challenges your memory as well, perhaps the following chart will help. Using the creation and the incarnation of Christ as the beginning and ending dates, we assign the eight eras to the closest five hundred year mark. To help you retain this information the chart associates the main Old Testament characters studied during this book.

ERA	1	2	3 and 4	5	7 and 8	New Testament Times
WHEN (approx.)	Creation	2000 BC	1500 BC	1000 BC	500 BC	Incarnation
WHO	Adam	Abraham	Moses and Joshua	David	Daniel and Ezra	Christ

Notice though that we omitted Era #6. We did not insert the Divided Era because King Hezekiah's reign occurred around 700 BC, falling almost exactly between 500 BC and 1000 BC.

WHO?

The main biblical characters we studied not only help us remember the general timing of each era, but also they help us to remember the lessons we learned that can help us grow spiritually.

BIBLICAL CHARACTER	FOUR AREAS OF SPIRITUAL GROWTH	EIGHT STEPS TO APPLY TO OUR LIVES
Adam	Fellowship with God	We must not hide our sin from God or blame it on others.
Abraham	Trust in God	We must not allow fear to paralyze us.
Moses	Obedience to God	We must not fail to follow-through on what God has commanded us to do.
Joshua	Hearing from God	We must not think just knowing the Bible is enough to be spiritually mature.
David	Fellowship with God	We must confess our sin honestly and immediately to God.
Hezekiah	Trust in God	We must make prayer our first choice, not our last chance.
Daniel	Obedience to God	We must obey God instantly regardless of the consequences.
Ezra	Hearing from God	We must set our hearts to study and practice what the Word of God teaches.

In many ways this section stands out from the others because we do not want to simply master the Word of God. We want it to master us. We can know the theme of Scripture, recite memory verses, and communicate with detail what takes place in each era, but if we do not obey Scripture's directives then it doesn't matter to God. He focuses far more on our hearts than He does our heads. We must learn from the people of Israel. (Twelve, ten, or two tribe Israel, it doesn't matter). God values transformation far more than information. Applying these eight spiritual growth steps to our lives will give God great pleasure.

WHY?

Over the course of the eight eras, we have exposed two misconceptions people often have about the Old Testament. First, people mistakenly believe that the Old Testament does not discuss the coming of Christ. Even though we examined only a few of the messianic prophecies, we have clearly seen that it does. In fact we have just scratched the surface since the Old Testament contains over three hundred prophecies of the future Messiah.

Many people, however, dismiss messianic prophecy with the rationalization that any charlatan could set himself up as the Christ by seeking to intentionally fulfill the existing prophecies. Take Zechariah 9:9 for example which prophesies the Messiah would come mounted on the foal of a donkey. Would it not be extremely easy for someone to ride a donkey into Jerusalem and declare himself to be the Christ? Of course! Yet no one could contrive the fulfillment of his own birth or death which Jesus did for both.

This leads to another objection. If all the prophecies of Christ could not be intentionally fulfilled by an imposter, then couldn't they be accidentally fulfilled? In other words, could it not have been just a coincidence that Christ fulfilled all the prophecies about Himself? For a discussion on the probability of someone fulfilling even a few of the prophecies about the coming Messiah, log on to www.geocities.com and read chapter 3 of a digital copy of the book *Science Speaks* by the famous mathematician Peter Stoner. He explains in laymen's terms that the probability of fulfilling only eight of the three hundred prophecies would be the same probability of covering the state of Texas two feet deep in silver dollars and having a blindfolded person pick a previously marked coin from all the others on his first try. He argues quite convincingly that Jesus Christ's fulfillment of the Old Testament prophecies could not have been a coincidence.

What about the second misconception people tend to have about the Old Testament? In this case we saw that people tend to incorrectly assume that in the Old Testament God's heart focuses only on the Hebrew race. This false thinking could not be further from the truth. From the beginning to the end of the Old Testament we find God's heart for the nations explicitly communicated in each of the eight eras. Consider the sampling found in the following chart.

ERA	SCRIPTURE	NATIONS OF THE EARTH
Nothing	Genesis 3:15	God shows His heart for the human race not just the Hebrew race
Something	Genesis 12:3	God wants to bless the Hebrews so that through them all the families of the earth will be blessed
Exiting	Exodus 19:4-6	God explains to the Hebrews that they are to serve as a kingdom of priests
Entering	Joshua 2:8-21	God allows a Gentile prostitute to become a forbearer of Christ
United	Psalm 67:1-2	The psalmist asks God to bless the Hebrews so that His salvation would be known among all nations
Divided	Isaiah 49:3,6	God declares that He has made Israel a light to the nations so that His salvation may reach to the ends of the earth
Scattered	Daniel 7:14	Daniel proclaims that all the peoples, nations, and men of every language would one day serve the Son of Man
Gathered	Zechariah 2:11	Zechariah predicts that many nations will join themselves to the Lord

We must not forget the book of Jonah, perhaps the clearest of all passages of God's heart for the nations. This Old Testament book focuses not on a whale, but on God as He sends one of His prophets to warn Assyria of His coming judgment. God loved the very nation that would one day slaughter His own people. Centuries later God demonstrated this same love toward the people whose sin would one day have His own Son sacrificed. Who were those sinful people? You and me.

Yet the story of Scripture centers not on you, me or any other person. The theme of Scripture stresses God receiving glory by restoring fellowship between the nations and Himself through His Son, Jesus Christ. We see this throughout the Historical books.

> *All the earth will be filled with the glory of the LORD.*
> *(Numbers 14:21)*

> *Tell of His glory among the nations, His wonderful deeds among*
> *all the peoples. Ascribe to the LORD, O families of the peoples,*
> *ascribe to the LORD glory and strength. Ascribe to the Lord the*
> *glory due His name. (1 Chronicles 16:24, 28, 29)*

We see this theme throughout the Poetical books.

> *Blessed be His glorious name forever; and may the whole earth be*
> *filled with His glory. (Psalm 72:19)*

> *Tell of His glory among the nations, his wonderful deeds among*
> *all the peoples. (Psalm 96:3)*

And we see the theme of God's glory throughout the Prophetical books.

> *Then the nations will bless themselves in Him, and in Him they*
> *will glory. (Jeremiah 4:2)*

> *For the earth will be filled with the knowledge of the glory of the*
> *LORD, as the waters cover the sea. (Habakkuk 2:14)*

For us to bring our lives into harmony with the emphasis of Scripture, we too must seek to bring Him glory. But how do we go about glorifying God? For starters we can begin to move beyond the *fact* that God has blessed us to the *reason* that God has blessed us. Just like He did with the people of the Old Testament, God has blessed us SO THAT we might be a blessing to others. We become a blessing to others by announcing not the coming Messiah, but the Messiah who has already come, Jesus Christ. Actively and intentionally participating in this great endeavor brings God immeasurable glory.

A LITTLE EXTRA

The chart on the following pages summarizes all we've looked at over the last eight chapters. It might help you if you made a copy of this chart and placed it in the front of your Bible. That way you will always have ready access to how to put together the puzzle of the Old Testament.

JUST FOR LAUGHS

The following list compiles conversations of children with God.

1. *Dear God, did you mean for giraffes to look like that or was that an accident? Norma, age 8*

2. *Dear God, in Bible times did they really talk that fancy? Jennifer, age 9*

3. *Dear God, please send Dennis to a different summer camp this year. Peter, age 7*

4. *Dear God, maybe Cain and Abel would not kill each other so much if they each had their own rooms. It works out ok with me and my brother. Larry, age 6*

5. *Dear God, I keep waiting for spring, but it never did come yet. What's up? Don't forget. Mark, age 7*

6. *Dear God, if you watch in church on Sunday I will show you my new shoes. Barbara, age 5*

7. *Dear God, is Reverend Coe a friend of yours, or do you just know him through the business? Donny, age 8*

8. *Dear God, I do not think anybody could be a better God than you. Well, I just want you to know that. I am not just saying that because you are already God. Charles, age 7*

9. *Dear God, it is great the way you always get the stars in the right place. Why can't you do that with the moon? Jeff, age 6*

ERA	NOTHING	SOMETHING	EXITING	ENTERING
SCRIPTURE	Genesis 1-11	Genesis 12-50	Exodus-Deut.	Joshua-Judges (Ruth)
WHAT?	Creating the human race	Choosing the Hebrew race	Delivering from Egypt	Conquering in Canaan
HOW?	4 Events: • creation • fall • flood • babel	4 Patriarchs: • Abraham • Isaac • Jacob • Joseph	4 Titles: • Exodus • Leviticus • Numbers • Deuteronomy	4 Steps: • sin • slavery • supplication • salvation
WHERE?	Fertile Crescent	Canaan	Egypt	Canaan
WHEN?	Creation–2090 BC	2090–1445 BC	1445–1405 BC	1405–1043 BC
WHO?	Adam	Abraham	Moses	Joshua
WHY?	Shows Christ coming to overcome sin/Satan (Gen. 3:15 ~ 1 Jn. 3:5-8)	Shows Christ coming from seed of Abraham (Gen. 12:2-3 ~ Gal. 3:16)	Shows Christ pictured as Passover Lamb (Ex. 12:13 ~ 1 Pt. 1:19)	Shows Christ pictured as scarlet cord (Joshua 2:15-22 ~ Heb. 11:31)
EXTRA	7 days of creation	12 tribes of Israel	10 commandments from God	12 judges of Israel

UNITED	DIVIDED	SCATTERED	GATHERED
1 Samuel- 1 Kings 11 (1 Chr. 1- 2 Chr. 9)	1 Kings 12- 2 Kings 23 (2 Chr. 10-35)	2 Kings 24-25 (2 Chr. 36)	Ezra-Nehemiah (Esther)
Prospering of nation	Separating into Israel & Judah	Exiling of Judah	Returning of Judah
3 Kings: • Saul • David • Solomon	3 Kingdoms: • Judah • Israel • Assyria	3 Departures: • Jehoiakim • Jehoiachin • Zedekiah	3 Returns: • Zerubbabel • Ezra • Nehemiah
Canaan	Canaan	Babylon	Canaan
1043–931 BC	931–722/586 BC	605–538 BC	538 BC–Christ
David	Hezekiah	Daniel	Ezra
Shows HOW Christ would die (Psalm 22 ~ Mt. 27:33- 50)	Shows WHY Christ would die (Isaiah 53:4-6 ~ 1 Pt. 2:21-25)	Shows WHEN Christ would die (Dan. 9:25 ~ Explained earlier)	Shows WHERE Christ would die (Zech. 9:9; 12:10 ~ Jn. 12:12-16; 19:37)
2 structures for worship	2 sets of kings/ prophets	6 empires of Old Testament	2 temples of Old Testament

APPENDIX ONE

APPENDIX ONE

THE RELIABILITY OF THE OLD TESTAMENT

During the days of the Old Testament when a scroll containing Scripture finally wore out, no one could replace it by simply printing another copy from their office computer. As with all ancient manuscripts, someone had to reproduce the desired copy by hand.

This fact understandably causes some sincere believers to ask, "How could the Old Testament with so many pages copied so many times by old men using candlelight without prescription glasses accurately reflect the original work?" Great question!

We can have confidence in the reliability of the Old Testament because of a special class of men called the scribes who developed in Jewish culture during the Babylonian exile. They made it their sole duty to preserve and transmit the Scripture with exactitude and precision. With meticulous care and fidelity, these men pledged themselves to fulfill stringent conditions in copying the Scriptures to ensure accuracy. What might appear as superfluous trivia in effect manifests the scribes' deep respect for the Scriptures. They made it a priority not to lose one jot (the smallest letter in Hebrew) or tittle (the smallest part of a letter) of the law.

Because the scribes followed such strict disciplines in regard to copying the Scriptures, when they finished transcribing a manuscript, their efforts convinced them that they had an exact duplicate. They confidently granted the new copy equal authority and buried or destroyed the old ones so no one would misunderstand the text through blurred or indistinct lettering.

So what steps did they take in the past to ensure that today we read a reliable version of the Old Testament?

- Out of reverence, the scribes did not write things down on just any kind of writing material, but only used the quality skin of a special kind of animal.

- The skin was prepared for use in a synagogue only by a Jewish scribe. (Not just anyone was allowed to copy.)

- The scroll was fastened together with strings from a special kind of animal.

- Each skin had to contain a specified number of columns equal throughout the entire book.

- The length of each column could not be less than 48 lines, or more than 60 lines.

- The column breadth had to consist of exactly 30 letters.

- They had to use a specially prepared recipe of black ink.

- They could only copy from an authentic copy, not a second edition.

- They copied nothing from memory.

- Between every consonant they left the breadth of one hair.

- Between every section they left the breadth of nine consonants.

- Between every book they left a space of three lines.

- The Pentateuch, the first five books of the Old Testament, had to terminate exactly with a line.

- The copyist had to sit in full Jewish dress.

- The scribes revered the Scripture and the name of God so much that a fresh quill would be used to pen the Lord's sacred name and the scribe could not acknowledge the presence of a king when writing that name.

- They had to produce a master copy.

Even with all this careful attention to accuracy, the scribes felt they could do more. So they also established the following checks and balances to ensure complete accuracy.

- They could copy only letter by letter. For example, they would look at the original, see a "T", copy a "T", see an "H", copy an "H", see an "E", copy an "E."

- As quality control, when a scribe finished a manuscript, another scribe would count the number of times each letter of the alphabet occurred in each book.

- He would also calculate the middle word.

- If more than three mistakes existed, the scribes would destroy the manuscript.

Imagine after going to so much trouble, your fellow scribe finds a fourth mistake on the last page. Talk about having a bad day. Just because the scribes went to such extremes, however, doesn't prove the copyists did their job. If we could somehow examine what we have today with a much earlier copy, then we could truly know the reliability of our Old Testament.

That's where archeology comes in. In 1947 a shepherd boy named Mohammed accidentally found a cave approximately eight miles from Jericho which contained several large sealed jars. Upon investigation, the locals discovered these sealed jars had preserved many ancient scrolls which we know today as the Dead Sea Scrolls due to the cave's proximity to the Dead Sea. Researchers dated one of the scrolls to the second century before the birth of Christ. Though minute variations in text did occur, not one of them changed the meaning of the passage since the differences were primarily in changes of spelling or letter strokes.

The significance of this find cannot be underestimated because it gives tremendous credibility to the reliability of the Old Testament we read today. Actually when compared to other documents of that time, no other manuscript even comes close in terms of accuracy of transmission. Thanks to Ezra and his fellow scribes, we can have complete confidence in the reliability of the Old Testament.

(Note: The above material comes from the leader's guide written by Bill Jones for the book and video entitled *Don't Check Your Brains at the Door,* authored by Josh McDowell.)

APPENDIX TWO

APPENDIX TWO

OLD TESTAMENT BOOK SUMMARIES

The charts found below list in order the thirty nine books of the Old Testament and briefly summarize the contents of each. The three charts correspond to the three corner pieces of the puzzle: the Historical, Poetical, and Prophetical books. By individualizing the charts for the various genres, more specific information can be communicated.

THE HISTORICAL BOOKS

BOOK	WHEN	WHAT	WHERE
Genesis	Nothing and Something Eras	Covers thousands of years of history beginning with the creation and fall of man, describes the flood and the origin of people groups, and ends with the stories of the four Hebrew patriarchs.	The Fertile Crescent, the Promised Land, and Egypt

BOOK	WHEN	WHAT	WHERE
Exodus	Exiting Era	Traces the Hebrews' departure from Egypt through the Red Sea to Mount Sinai where they receive the Ten Commandments and instructions for building their Tabernacle.	Egypt and Mount Sinai
Leviticus	Exiting Era	Focuses on five offerings and seven feasts that the Levite priests use to worship God.	Mount Sinai
Numbers	Exiting Era	Begins with Moses counting the Hebrews then leading them to the edge of the Promised Land before wandering in the wilderness for years until they come to Moab where Moses counts them again.	Mount Sinai, the edge of the Promised Land, the wilderness, and Moab
Deuteronomy	Exiting Era	Tells of Moses giving the Ten Commandments again to the Hebrews before he dies and they march into the Promised Land.	Moab at the edge of the Promised Land
Joshua	Entering Era	Explains how Joshua leads the Hebrews into the Promised Land and conquers the Canaanites physically.	The Promised Land
Judges	Entering Era	Describes how the Canaanites conquer the Hebrews spiritually and how God repeatedly sends a deliverer to set them free from their physical and spiritual bondage.	The Promised Land
Ruth	Entering Era	Portrays the beautiful love story between Boaz and Ruth, a non-Hebrew, whose marriage resulted in the forefathers of King David and ultimately Jesus Christ.	The Promised Land

BOOK	WHEN	WHAT	WHERE
1 Samuel	United Era	Shows the transition from the leadership of judges to the rule of kings by telling the stories of Samuel, King Saul, and introducing the shepherd boy David who slays Goliath the giant.	The Promised Land
2 Samuel	United Era	Deals with the reign of King David, specifically his conquests, compromise with Bathsheba and Uriah, and his resulting consequences.	The Promised Land
1 Kings	United and Divided Eras	Recalls how God divides the nation of Israel into the northern and southern kingdoms because Solomon turns his heart from God to worship the idols of his many foreign wives.	The Promised Land, then alternates between the northern and southern kingdoms
2 Kings	Divided and Scattered Eras	Communicates the sad story of how God sends Assyria to conquer the northern kingdom because they continued to worship the golden calves and how God sends Babylon to conquer the southern kingdom because they followed the sins of Manasseh.	Alternates between the Northern and Southern kingdoms, Babylon
1 Chronicles	United Era	Highlights first the ancestry then the activity of King David.	The Promised Land
2 Chronicles	United, Divided, and Scattered Eras	Starts with the reign of Solomon but after God divides the nation, focuses only on the southern kingdom until Nebuchadnezzar carries the people of Judah into exile.	The Promised Land, Judah, Babylon

BOOK	WHEN	WHAT	WHERE
Ezra	Gathered Era	Speaks first of Zerubbabel returning from exile to the Promised Land to reconstruct the temple and then of Ezra returning to the Jerusalem to reform the people.	Persia, the Promised Land
Nehemiah	Gathered Era	Ends recorded Old Testament history by relating the third return from exile to Jerusalem where Nehemiah rebuilds the city's defensive walls.	Persia, the Promised Land
Esther	Gathered Era	Dwells on God's protection of the exiles as He promotes a Jewish woman named Esther to queen of the Persians where she foils a plot to eliminate all the Jews.	Persia

THE POETICAL BOOKS

BOOK	WHEN	WHAT	WHO
Job	Nothing or Something Era	Examines the topic of suffering and why God allows bad things to happen to good people.	Author unknown
Psalms	United Era	Directs the reader in praise and worship to the character and works of the Living God.	David (seventy-three of them), Asaph (50,73-83), Sons of Korah (42, 44-49, 84, 85, 87), Solomon (72, 127), Heman (88), Ethan (89), Moses (90), and anonymous (fifty of them)

BOOK	WHEN	WHAT	WHO
Proverbs	United Era	Provides instruction through hundreds of wise statements on how to live life successfully from God's perspective.	Solomon, Agur (30), and Lemuel (31)
Ecclesiastes	United Era	Talks about the insignificance of everything done under the sun versus the meaning found in life when viewed from "above the sun."	Solomon
Song of Solomon	United Era	Describes Solomon falling in love and marrying a poor non-Hebrew shepherdess.	Solomon

THE PROPHETICAL BOOKS

BOOK	WHEN	WHAT	WHY
Isaiah	Divided Era	Predicts in chapter 39 that Judah will be defeated and taken captive by Babylon, but ends with the assurance of future restoration.	Alas, sinful nation, people weighed down with iniquity, offspring of evildoers, sons who act corruptly! They have abandoned the LORD, they have despised the Holy One of Israel, they have turned away from Him (Isaiah 1:4).

BOOK	WHEN	WHAT	WHY
Jeremiah	Divided Era	Pleads with Judah to repent before the Babylonians carry the people into exile by issuing "words which came from the Lord."	And the Lord has sent to you all His servants the prophets again and again, but you have not listened nor inclined your ear to hear, saying, "Turn now everyone from his evil way and from the evil of your deeds, and dwell on the land which the Lord has given to you and your forefathers forever and ever; and do not go after other gods to serve them and to worship them. . . ." Yet you have not listened (Jeremiah 25:4-7).
Lamentations	Divided Era	Jeremiah mourns for the siege and destruction of Jerusalem by the Babylonians in five dirges each contained in one of the book's five chapters.	Judah has gone into exile under affliction and under harsh servitude; she dwells among the nations . . . (Lamentations 1:3).
Ezekiel	Scattered Era	Prophesies in chapters 4-24 from Babylon (having gone there as part of the second group of exiles) about the ultimate fall of Jerusalem structuring his messages around the phrase "the word of the Lord came to me, saying" (6:1, 7:1, 11:14, 12:1, 12:8, 12:17, 12:21, 12:26, 13:1, 14:2, 14:12, 15:1, 16:1, 17:1, 17:11, 18:1, 20:2, 20:45, 21:1, 21:8, 21:18, 22:1, 22:17, 22:23, 23:1, 24:1, 24:15).	Then He said to me, "Son of man, I am sending you to the sons of Israel, to a rebellious people who have rebelled against Me; they and their fathers have transgressed against Me to this very day" (Ezekiel 2:3).

BOOK	WHEN	WHAT	WHY
Daniel	Scattered Era	Communicates hope in chapters 8-12 from Babylon (having gone there as part of the first group of exiles) about the future of God's captive people using three visions (8, 9, and 10-12).	Now I [a divine messenger] have come to give you [Daniel] an understanding of what will happen to your people in the latter days, for the vision pertains to the days yet future (Daniel 10:14).
Hosea	Divided Era	Compares the physical adultery of his wife in the first three chapters to the spiritual adultery of the northern kingdom toward God in the last eleven chapters and as a consequence of Assyria's conquest.	My people consult their wooden idol, and their diviner's wand informs them; for a spirit of harlotry has led them astray, and they have played the harlot, departing from their God. . . . They will not return to the land of Egypt; but Assyria . . . will be their king, because they refused to return to Me (Hosea 4:12, 11:5).
Joel	Divided Era	Calls the southern kingdom of Judah to repent in order to avert the day of the Lord's judgment in the form of Babylon's army which he compares to a recent locust plague and drought.	Blow a trumpet in Zion, and sound an alarm on My holy mountain! Let all the inhabitants of the land tremble, for the day of the LORD is coming; surely it is near, a day of darkness and gloom. . . . So there is a great and mighty people; there has never been anything like it, nor will there be again after it to the years of many generations. . . . "Yet even now," declares the LORD, "Return to Me with all your heart." . . . But I will remove the northern army far from you (Joel 2:1, 2, 12, 20).

BOOK	WHEN	WHAT	WHY
Amos	Divided Era	Sounds the alarm for the northern kingdom to repent of their sins before it is too late by using three messages in chapters 3 to 5 starting with the phrase "Hear this word" (3:1, 4:1, 5:1) and four visions in chapters 7 and 8 beginning with the phrase "Thus the Lord God showed me" (7:1, 7:4, 7:7, 8:1).	You only have I chosen among all the families of the earth; therefore, I will punish you for all your iniquities (Amos 3:2).
Obadiah	Divided Era	Condemns Edom, the nation which descended from Jacob's brother Esau, for harassing the Hebrews over the generations which began with not helping the Hebrews while they wandered in the wilderness.	Because of violence to your brother Jacob, you will be covered with shame, and you will be cut off forever (Obadiah 1:10).
Jonah	Divided Era	Warns Nineveh, the capital of Assyria, to repent resulting in a great spiritual revival.	Arise, go to Nineveh the great city, and cry against it, for their wickedness has come up before Me (Jonah 1:2).

BOOK	WHEN	WHAT	WHY
Micah	Divided Era	Explains the causes for Judah's future Babylonian captivity, but adds the promise of her future return.	[Jerusalem's] leaders pronounce judgment for a bribe, her priests instruct for a price and her prophets divine for money. Yet they lean on the LORD saying, "Is not the LORD in our midst? Calamity will not come upon us." Therefore, on account of you . . . Jerusalem will become a heap of ruins, and the mountain of the temple will become high places of a forest. . . . For now you will go out of the city, dwell in the field, and go to Babylon. There you will be rescued; there the LORD will redeem you from the hand of your enemies (Micah 3:11,12; 4:10).
Nahum	Divided Era	Announces the future destruction of Nineveh describing both how and why God's judgment on Assyria will occur which brings relief to Judah who is threatened by this powerful and wicked nation.	The LORD has issued a command concerning you [Nineveh]: "Your name will no longer be perpetuated. I will cut off idol and image from the house of your gods. I will prepare your grave, for you are contemptible" (Nahum 1:14).
Habakkuk	Divided Era	Questions God (1:2-4) about why He does not judge Judah's iniquity and then when God answers that He will use Babylon to discipline Judah, Habakkuk questions God again (1:12-17) as to why He would use a nation more wicked than Judah for that purpose.	Question: Why do You make me see iniquity and cause me to look on wickedness? Answer: "Look among the nations! Observe! Be astonished! Wonder! Because I am doing something in your days—you would not believe if you were told. For behold, I am raising up the Chaldeans [Babylonians] . . . " (Habakkuk 1:3-6).

BOOK	WHEN	WHAT	WHY
Zephaniah	Divided Era	Uses the phrase "the day of the Lord" twenty times in thirteen verses (1:7-10, 14-16, 18; 2:2-3; 3:8,11,16) to describe God's coming judgment upon sin, Judah's specifically and the nations' generally.	Seek the LORD, all you humble of the earth who have carried out His ordinances; seek righteousness, seek humility. Perhaps you will be hidden in the day of the LORD's anger (Zephaniah 2:3).
Haggai	Gathered Era	Rebukes the people who have returned from the Babylonian captivity for not finishing the rebuilding of the temple by preaching four messages, each precisely dated (1:1; 2:1; 2:10; 2:20).	Thus says the LORD of hosts, "This people says, 'The time has not come, even the time for the house of the LORD to be rebuilt'" (Haggai 1:2).
Zechariah	Gathered Era	Encourages the people who have returned from the Babylonian captivity to finish building the temple using eight visions (1:8; 1:18; 2:1; 3:1; 4:2; 5:1; 5:5; 6:1), four announcements (7:4,8; 8:1,18) and two burdens (9:1; 12:1).	This is the word of the LORD to Zerubbabel saying, "Not by might nor by power, but by My Spirit," says the LORD. . . . "The hands of Zerubbabel have laid the foundation of this house, and his hands will finish it" (Zechariah 4:6,9).
Malachi	Gathered Era	Exposes the sinful practices of both the priests (1:2; 1:6; 1:7; 1:13) and people (2:10; 2:14; 2:17; 3:7; 3:8; 3:13) of Judah using a series of accusations and rhetorical questions.	"I am not pleased with you," says the LORD of hosts, "nor will I accept an offering from you" (Malachi 1:10).

Please note that since the above charts limit the prophetical book summaries to only one sentence, they have stressed only the historical context in order to reinforce the eight eras studied in this book. Unfortunately, this limitation results in the ignoring of vast numbers of references where the prophets also stress God's faithful concern for His people and the coming Messiah. We must remember that, out of love, God judged His people's disobedience in order to win them back to fellowship, not pay them back.

Crossover, an international church planting movement, intensely desires to see God glorified among all the peoples of the world. Founded in 1987 by Dr. Bill Jones (President, Crossover – USA) and Jason Butler (President, Crossover – Brazil), today Crossover serves on all six continents and has planted many churches among the least reached peoples of the world.

Crossover mobilizes church planters from sending bases in four countries: Australia, Brazil, Moldova and the USA. This international partnership and cross-cultural dynamic helps us accomplish more for the expansion of God's Kingdom than we could separately. Our common vision and values hold us together as we passionately seek to multiply church planters to plant multiplying churches among the least reached peoples of the world.

If you would like additional information on Crossover, the author, ways in which to become directly involved in our movement or to order additional books, please contact us at 803-691-0688 or visit our web site: www.crossoverusa.org.

CROSSOVER
COMMUNICATIONS
INTERNATIONAL